CISTERCIAN FATHERS SERIES: NUMBER FOURTY-EIGHT

SERLO OF SAVIGNY AND SERLO OF WILTON

SEVEN UNPUBLISHED WORKS

Serlo of Savigny and Serlo of Wilton
SEVEN UNPUBLISHED WORKS

Edited and translated by

† LAWRENCE C. BRACELAND, SJ

CISTERCIAN PUBLICATIONS

KALAMAZOO, MICHIGAN

1988

This book has been published with the help of a grant from the Canadian Federation for the Humanities, using funds provided by the Social Sciences and Humanities Research Council of Canada.

The work of Cistercian Publications is made possible in part by support from Western Michigan University to the Institute of Cistercian Studies.

Available in Britain and Europe from

A. R. Mowbray & Co Ltd
St Thomas House   Becket Street
Oxford OX1 1Sj

Available elsewhere (including Canada)
from the publisher

Cistercian Publications
WMU Station
Kalamazoo, Michigan 49008

Library of Congress Cataloguing in Publication Data:

Seven unpublished works.

(Cistercian Fathers series; no. 48)
Bibliography: pp xiii-xxiii
Includes indexes.
Contents: Peter and Paul, two olive trees; Commandments and plagues; A prelate, the fruit of an olive tree/Serlo of Savigny—For the just, all's well; For and against the Lord; The great supper; The Lord's prayer/Serlo of Wilton.
1. Christian literature, English—Translations from Latin. 2. Christian literature, Latin—Translations into English. I. Serlo, Abbot of Savigny, d. 1158. II. Serlo, of Wilton, ca. 1110–1181.
III. Braceland, Lawrence C. IV. Series.
BR53.S45   1987   242   87–17864
ISBN 0–87907–048–X

Typeset by Solaris Press II   *Printed in the United States of America*

To Very Reverend William Michael Addley

Provincial of the Upper Canadian Jesuits

who for more than a decade supported my research

into the writings of twelfth-century cistercian abbots

Qui parentes non ueneratur
merito pena canum multatur
Serlo of Savigny

Ipsa ruina est medicina
Serlo of Wilton

Father Lawrence Braceland SJ died on 1 March 1987, before having had an opportunity to proofread the galleys of this book. While great care has been taken to ensure that his painstaking work is presented as he intended, we realize that the work existed in design and detail principally in Father Larry's mind, and we are therefore conscious of being deprived of his attentiveness at this crucial stage. We are grateful to Dr Francis R. Swietek for carefully proofing the latin texts and their apparatus.

Father Braceland entered the Society of Jesus in 1929, and took up Cistercian studies on his (semi) retirement from active teaching. His graceful translations of the works of Gilbert of Hoyland, of Aelred of Rievaulx, and now of the two Serlos, and the learned and lively papers he presented each year at the Kalamazoo Cistercian Studies Conference attest to his great love and mastery of language and scholarship, his generosity, and, above all, his love of God.

E. R. E

ACKNOWLEDGEMENTS

I am grateful to St Paul's College, the University of Manitoba and the Canadian Federation of the Humanities for travel grants to allow the presentation of papers annually at Kalamazoo, Michigan. For a grant-in-aid of publication I wish also to thank the Canadian Federation of the Humanities, using funds provided by the Social Sciences and Humanities Research Council of Canada.

In appropriate places with the microfilms or copies of manuscripts they have provided, I have acknowledged the help of others. But so many librarians and archivists have come to my aid, that I fear I may forget more than one. Let me acknowledge especially the continuing encouragement of Fr Leonard Boyle, OP, now Vatican Librarian, the advice of Dr Francis R. Swietek, and the editorial assistance of Dr Rozanne Elder.

L.C.B

CONTENTS

INTRODUCTION

THE PUBLICATION OF THESE SEVEN WORKS of two early cistercian abbots, I hope, may hasten the presentation of definitive lives and works of both these important abbots. Of the seven works presented here, the first three belong to Serlo of Savigny (d. 1158), the fourth more probably to Serlo of Wilton, and the last three certainly to Serlo of Wilton (or of Aumône, d. 1181).

SAVIGNY

Savigny was noted for a holiness which knew no bounds. Did it not show how sanctity can flourish in fens, prairies and forests? And is it accidental that these lines are being written in a cosmopolitan canadian parish, whose patron is St Vital, either the roman centurion or the norman founder of the Congregation of Savigny? Can it be fortuitous that the local pastor is one of seven priests in a bilingual family, who with their mother were invited to share the Eucharist and a papal breakfast with his Holiness, John Paul II? Or is it providential that this short account is being composed a stone's throw away from the original site of the cistercian abbey, The Prairies, recently removed to Holland, Manitoba? Accidents and providence are written large in the story of Savigny.

Two abbots named Serlo, from different countries by varied routes, entered a congregation which followed the benedictine Rule and became a center of monastic reform at the end of the eleventh century. Vitalis of Mortain (d. 1122) the founding father, resigned as canon of the collegiate church of St Evroul, in the diocese of Lisieux. In his search for greater solitude, he joined a number of hermits living in scattered huts in a forest called in contemporary sources 'a new Egypt'. In 1105, he entered the forest of Savigny, on the confines of Normandy and Brittany, where he built a hermitage. The growing number of his disciples suggested the construction of adequate buildings in which monastic life could begin and flourish according to the Rule of St Benedict. There the form of visitation and general chapters closely resembled the organization of Cîteaux and with the assistance of lay brothers the emphasis was placed on agricultural labor.

Within thirty years of its inception, thanks to the number of new foundations, Savigny became the head of an influential congregation

Introduction

numbering thirty-three subordinate houses. Under Geoffrey, who succeeded Vital, King Henry I of England established and generously endowed twenty-nine Savigniac monasteries in his dominions. Serlo, the fourth abbot general, was fascinated by the magnetism of Bernard of Clarivaux. Despite opposition from within his own congregation, in 1147 he brought all the houses of the grey monks, not to mention the grey nuns, into the magnetic cistercian field. 'Savigny was given a place in the Cistercian hierarchy immediately after the four "elder daughters," and the abbot was permitted to have three horses in his equipage.'[1]

In *Moyen Age*, Jacqueline Buhot gave a brief history of the congregation, 'L'Abbaye normande de Savigny'. In *Revue Mabillon*, Dom Léon Guilloreau recounted the story of the english foundations, 'Les Fondations anglaises de l'Abbaye de Savigny', and in *The American Benedictine Review*, Professor Bennet Hill related, 'The beginnings of the First French Foundations of the Norman Abbey of Savigny'. According to Francis Swietek and Terrence Deneen, 'These Savigniacs were praised effusively by contemporaries as models to be followed. In spite of Savigny's acknowledged importance, however, many aspects of its early history remain relatively unstudied'.[2]

SERLO OF SAVIGNY

For October 20th, the feastday of Blessed Serlo of Savigny, the Bollandist Victor de Buck, in the *Acta Sanctorum*, sifted the records for a brief presentation of the life and work of Serlo of Savigny. A native of Vaubadon in the department of Calvados, Serlo entered the benedictine abbey of Cerisy and in 1113 transferred to Savigny, whose abbot he was to become in 1140. As Abbot General of this important congregation, he found it difficult to retain his juristiction over the monasteries in England, which preferred independence. Hence Serlo determined to affiliate the congregation to the Order of Cîteaux and step by step this was completed in 1147–48. Several weeks before the death of St Bernard of Clairvaux in 1153, Serlo abdicated from Savigny and retired to Bernard's monastery, where he died on 10 September 1158. After reviewing the pertinent manuscripts in *Revue Mabillon*, Fr André Wilmart listed thirty-four writings of Serlo of Savigny. With Fr DeBuck and others, he attributed an exposition on the *Our Father* not to Serlo of *Savigny* but to Serlo of Wilton.[3]

SERLO OF WILTON OR OF AUMÔNE

Serlo of Wilton was born some five miles from Salisbury in England. This wandering scholar became known as teacher and master, *gram[m]aticus* and *magister*. He has his place among the leading secular and religious lyricists of his day. After being exiled from England to a port on the Mediterranean, probably to Antibes, he was recalled to lecture first at the University of Paris and then at the *studium generale* in Oxford. Upon his conversion at Oxford, he became the paradigm of the contrite monk, first at the cluniac monastery of La charité-sur-Loire, and then at the more austere cistercian monastery of Aumône in Normandy, where he became abbot. His death is recorded in the Annals of Waverley, near Farnham, in Surrey, in 1181 – not surprisingly, since Waverley was a daughter-house of Aumône in the line of Cîteaux.

His definitive biography is long overdue. His poetic works have now been edited and published. His proverbs, 1150–1170, were presented by Professor A. C. Friend in *Mediaeval Studies*, Toronto. His latin verses were disentangled from the verses of two namesakes, Serlo of Bayeux (d. about 1200) and Serlo of Fountains (about 1109–1209), by Professor Jan Öberg, in *Studia Latina Stockholmiensia*, 1965. In listing a number of prose theological works attributed to a Serlo, not clearly identified, Professor Öberg gave some momentum to the attempt to identify the author of those works.[4]

MANUSCRIPTS OF SERLO OF SAVIGNY

Using MS Troyes 1771, (V) ff. 1–70v, Fr Bertrand Tissier published the works of Serlo of Savigny, but omitted numbers 15, 25, 26, 33, 34, of André Wilmart's subsequent list. Using what he considered the better MS, Troyes 227 (C), ff. 117v–132v, collated with Troyes 1771 (V), ff. 1r–70v, and Paris B. N. 2681A (B) ff. 108r–196v, Wilmart edited a work omitted by Tissier, number 25 of Wilmart's list, as a good illustration of Serlo's matter and manner. Wilmart also called attention to another MS, Paris B. N. Latin 2594, f. 11v–12r, which contains sermon no. 18, in Wilmart's list, already published by Tissier.[5]

One excerpt in *Jesus College MS 19, f. 12, c. 2* (J) should be added here. Three excerpts of Serlo of Savigny are found in this MS from the end of the thirteenth century, of unknown origin, and kept in the Bodleian

Library, Oxford. The first excerpt, ff. 12r, cc. 1–2, *Hec duo genera . . . isti quiescunt in contemplatione,* is found in Tissier, p. 112, c. *Sermo 1, in festo S. Ioannis Baptiste.* The third excerpt, *Iusti tulerunt spolia impiorum . . . sed diuine potestati ascribendum est,* is also found in Tissier, p. 122, cc. 1–2, at the beginning of *Sermo 4, De omnibus sanctis.* The second excerpt, however, f. 12, c. 2, *Item, De oliueto prelatus sumi debeat non spineto,* was not published by Tissier nor mentioned by Wilmart, nor have I found it elsewhere.[6]

Hence five unpublished pieces are attributed to Serlo of Savigny, two incorrectly, in the following MSS:

1) *Wilmart 15,* B, ff. 131v–134v; C, ff. 122r, c. 2–122v, c. 2; V, ff. 50r–52v. In a sermon for the feast of Peter and Paul, 30 June, Serlo skilfully illustrates the apostles' life and death through the symbolism of a passage in the Apocalypse (11:4–7).

2) *Wilmart 26,* B, ff. 164r–167v; C. ff. 129, c. 2–129v, c. 2; V, ff. 61v–64v. Preaching to the people at Rheims, Serlo comments on the two musical instruments of praise: the cithara and the psaltery.

> *Wilmart 33;* V, Troyes 1771, ff. 48v–49r. In this short note on the word *Respexit* in the *Magnificat* the author explains that God regards us with understanding, grace, and judgement. This note, however, is in fact an excerpt from Hugh of St Victor, *Explanatio in canticum beatae Mariae,* (PL 175: 422C–423A) beginning and ending *Respexit humilitatem ancillae suae,* i.e. 421D–422C. Although attributed to Serlo it was rightly omitted from Tissier's edition. Let me thank Professor Francis R. Swietek, The University of Dallas, for calling this to my attention.
>
> *Wilmart 34;* V, Troyes 1771, 48v–49r. In a short note *Quattuor,* the author explains that four steps: reading, meditation, prayer, and good work *(operatio),* lead to the top step of perfection, contemplation. This note is chapter 9 of book V of the *Didascalicon,* of Hugh of St Victor (see ed. of C. H. Buttimer, pp. 109–111) and was omitted from Tissier's edition. Despite the MS and André Wilmart, Professor Swietek saved me from another error.

3) *Add to Wilmart, no. 35:* J, Oxford, Bodley, Jesus College ms. 19, f. 12, c. 2: the qualities expected of a prelate chosen by the people, are indicated through the symbols of the text.

4)   *Master Serlo in Windsor, Eton College* MS. *39*

Another sermon, attributed to *Magister Serlo* is here listed between three
certain works of Serlo of Savigny and three certain works of Serlo of
Wilton. Fuller examination may help to discover to which of the two it
belongs. According to the catalogue of Professor N. R. Ker (1972),
Windsor, Eton College MS 39, belongs to the early thirteenth century.
All but one of its entries are attributed to Bernard of Clairvaux (d. 1153).
The one exception is attributed to *Magister Serlo.* The first work is Bernard's *De consideratione,* written for the cistercian Pope, Eugenius III. The
second, also attributed to Bernard of Clairvaux at the beginning and the
end, is entitled *De Amore Dei.* However, this is in fact two works now
ascribed to William of St Thierry (d. 1148): *De contemplando deo* and *De
natura et dignitate amoris.* Contrary to an earlier suggestion, the last
fourty-eight pieces belong not to Gilbert of Hoyland but to Bernard of
Clairvaux.

In the MS, all references to Bernard before f. 61v, c. 2, give him the title Blessed, but from that column to the last, he is called Saint, a title of-
ficially conferred in 1174, and promulgated to the Cistercians in their
general chapter of 1175 (SBOp 1: xxiv, and footnote 3). From this
change of Blessed to Saint, one would assume that, if not Eton College
MS 39, then its original was being written about 1174–75. In the top left-
hand margin of folio 46v, a reference to Isaiah 3:10, *ys 3.c,* is in a later
hand; the verse number *c,* for this entry indicates a date after 1230, when
verses in Scripture began to be numbered from *a* to *g,* like notes in a
musical scale.

In the rubric and at the foot of folio 46v, is the title: *Sermo Magistri
Serlonis de iusto homine bene uiuente.* Neither Tissier nor Wilmart claimed
the work for Serlo of Savigny. In *Traditio* 8 (1952) p. 416, Dr C. H.
Talbot listed the folios as 46–59 instead of 46v–48r, and attributed the
sermon to Serlo of Savigny. Indeed Serlo of Savigny would seem more
at home with Bernard and William than Serlo of Wilton. At lines
12–13, a rhyme catches the ear: *ipsa ruina . . . est medicina.* Although the
rhetorical style, the title *Magister,* and the citation of Isidore of Seville
suggest Serlo of Wilton, they do not exclude Serlo of Savigny. The ap-
pearance of this sermon of *Magister Serlo,* the only unpublished piece in
the manuscript, is long overdue.

5)   *London B. M., Sloane* MS. *2478, 73r–75v*

In another rich MS, London, B. M., Sloane MS 2478, two further sermons are attributed to *Magister* Serlo. One is for the third Sunday of
Lent, as indicated in the MS, and the other, to judge by the text, Lk
14:16, is for the second Sunday after Pentecost. The first, ff. 73r–75v,
on the text of Lk 11:23: 'one who is not with me, is against me', treats
the virtues and commandments. The second, ff. 82r–83v, on the text of
Lk 14:16, 'a man spread a great supper', discusses the banquet of heaven.
In addition to the title, some verses suggest that the author is the gram-
marian and poet, Serlo of Wilton. To distinguish various species of oaths
the author introduces into the text two riming hexameters:

> *Si male iurandi sit cura notandi:*
> *per primas fato, per ydonea commemorato.*

He first explains the mnemonic in the word *fato*: the letter *f* stands for a
false oath, and the letter *a* the appetite for oaths. Then through the letters of the word *ydonea*, he lists the species of perverse oaths: the *y* or *i*
stands for an impetuous oath; *d* for a dolorous, *o* for an otiose, *e* for an
erroneous, and *a* for an assiduous oath. In a letter of 9 May, 1983, Jan
Öberg, the editor of Serlo's verse, says this is 'quite in the vein of Serlo of
Wilton'.

At the foot of f. 74v, apparently in the same hand, the ten commandments are summarized in four hexameters:

> *Ydola sperne, dei nomen tibi non sit inane.*
> *Sabbata sanctifices. Habeas in honore prantes.*
> *Non occisor eris, mechus, fur, testis iniquus.*
> *Non aliam nuptas, non res cupias alienas.*

Although in the same letter Professor Öberg remarks that these are 'only
incomplete one-syllable rhymes', they are lines likely to have lingered in
the memory of a monk who had been a wandering scholar.

In the fourth commandment, says Master Serlo, we obey our spiritual
father and mother, and prelates of the church. Here Serlo is severely and
abundantly scriptural, though he quotes Ambrose to the effect that one
who does not feed the starving is guilty of killing them and cites the gloss to
define a theft as 'filching what belongs to another against that other's will'.

At the foot of folio 74r, apparently in the same hand, are given in rhyme these distinctions about rejoicing:

$$\text{Gaudete:} \begin{cases} \textit{in domino, non in seculo,} \\ \textit{in ueritate, non in iniquitate,} \\ \textit{in spe eternitatis, non in flore uanitatis.} \end{cases}$$

Professor Öberg comments in the same letter that this 'does not resemble anything in the Serlo works known to me'. Finally, Serlo sums up the commandments in the words of Isidore of Seville and compares them to the ten-stringed psalter according to Augustine. Gregory the Great and Ambrose are quoted in the margin. The sermon, both instructive and attractive, could be claimed for Serlo of Wilton by virtue of the title, *Magister*, the mnemonic, and the verses in the text, although the verses at the foot of ff. 74v and 75r, are probably not by Serlo of Wilton.

6)   *London B. M., Sloane* MS *2478, ff. 82r–83v*

In the second sermon of *Magister* Serlo in this MS, ff. 82r–83v, heaven is compared to the final banquet, to the net cast into the sea to catch large fish, and to the wedding feast. Here Serlo relies more heavily on the Fathers, whom he quotes in the gloss, in the interlinear, and in the available manuscripts: Ambrose, Augustine, Bede, and Gregory the Great many times. One passage has an interesting pedigree. The servant sent repeatedly to invite reluctant guests, is compared to an order of preachers: *mittitur seruus quasi ordo predicatorum ad inuitatos*. This refers neither to the Franciscans, approved as an order by Innocent III in 1209, nor to the Dominicans founded at Toulouse in 1215. The passage, quoted in the *gloss ordinaria* on Lk 14:16 (PL 114:308), and in Bede (PL 92:514B), derives from Gregory I (PL 76:1267B) who refers to himself as a member of an order of preachers (Augustinians).

The title *Magister* common to both sermons, their proximity in the MS, the verses and mnemonics in the former, and the more extensive use of the Fathers and the gloss in both, suggest that they should be included in the works of Serlo of Wilton. The spelling and punctuation, which I have tried to retain, resemble those of Eton College MS 39. Quotation-marks, paragraphs, and the enumeration of both lines and paragraphs, have been added. In the MS, numbers for the chapters in scripture are set off by periods. In the first sermon, the roman numerals for the commandments are introduced into the text from the margins.

Z)   *Oxford, Bodleian, Laud Misc. 112*

Jan Öberg likewise called attention to a penitential work, *Summa magistri Scerle de penitentia*, in the Bodleian Library, Oxford, Laud Misc., MS 112, ff. 398v–407v. Professor Öberg gives evidence that the name Scerle is a variant spelling for Serlo. This penitential was published with commentary in *Mediaeval Studies* 38 (1976) pp. 1–53, and 40 (1978) pp. 290–311, by Professor Joseph W. Goering, who dated the MS after 1234, but did not identify the author. Is it possible that in this MS, an earlier work of an author called *Magister* Serlo, who held earlier views, was updated with quotations from the work of Raymond of Pennafort after AD 1234? Is Serlo of Wilton eliminated as the author of this earlier work, *Summa magistri Scerle de penitentia?*[10]

Six sermons therefore are attributed either to Serlo of Savigny or to Serlo of Wilton. For these six, the spelling and punctuation follow the MSS. Nevertheless, the punctuation does require some adaptation: dots on the line become periods; dots above the line commas; dots topped by what look like an arabic 7, are rendered by semi-colons; dots topped by check marks (√) are rendered by colons. Once a question mark needs to be rendered by an exclamation-mark. Quotation marks are added. Scriptural references, enumeration of lines and paragraphs are introduced for reference. However, for the seventh and final work, because of the numerous MSS, a more modern punctuation was adopted.

7)   *Manuscripts of Serlo's Exposition on the Lord's Prayer*

At least twenty-two MSS have preserved an interesting exposition of the Lord's Prayer by *Magister* Serlo. The following abbreviations will facilitate reference to the MSS: each is followed by the MS number and folio pages, and where available, the source, ascription, date, and so on:

A — Admont, Austria, Stiftsbibliothek-Stiftsarchiv, Benedictinerstift, MS 82, ff. 213v–216v, XII, *Serlo*, reproduced thanks to Dr Johann Tomaschek of Admont and to Dr Julian G. Plante of the Hill Monastic Manuscript Library, Collegeville.

AU — Auxerre, France, Bibliothèque Municipale, MS 20, ff. 151r–155v, XIV–XV, Celestins de Sens, *Anon*, microfilmed thanks to Mme. M. Michaud of Auxerre and to the Centre National de la Recherche Scientifique, (CNRS), Paris.

BE — Berlin, Germany, Staatsbibliothek (Preussischer Kulturbesitz), MS lat. oct. 375, ff. 32r–37v, XV *exeunte*, S. Augustini Canones, Bodeken *apud* Paderborn, *Anon, accessum* 1933 *ex Cheltenham*, Phillips MS 697; microfilmed thanks to Ch. Dickman, Berlin.

B — Brussels, Belgium, Bibliothèque Royale, II 1066 (cat. 3065), ff. 183v–185v, XIII, Sancte Marie De Alna, *Serlo;* f. 1, *ex libris* 4646 Ph(illips), *acquisitum ex bibliotheca Cheltenham anno* 1888, microfilmed thanks to the Bibliothèque Royale Albert 1 er.

C — Cambridge, England, Corpus Christi College, MS 62 (Sub d. 8), ff. 129r–131r, XII (N. R. Ker, *Medieval Libraries*, p. 160), Rochester, OSB, *Serlo, donum per Alkewinum monachum* (Ker, p. 160), microfilmed thanks to The Librarian, Master and Fellows of Corpus Christi College, Cambridge.

D — Dijon, France, Bibliothèque Publique, MS 42 (24) ff. 174r, c. 1 to 181r, c. 2, XII *exeunte*, Cîteaux, *Anon*, microfilmed thanks to P. Gras of Dijon, Anne-Véronique Gilles and the CNRS, Paris.

E — Evreux, France, Bibliothèque Municipale, MS 41, ff. 70r–75r, XIII, Abbaye de Lyre, *Exposicio Serlonis abbatis de Elemosina*, reproduced thanks to the Librarian, M. De Grave, Evreux.

G — Graz, Austria, Universitätsbibliothek, MS 453, ff. 59v–63v, XIII *exeunte*, Serlo, reproduced thanks to Dr Hans Zotter, Graz, and Dr Julian G. Plante, Hill Monastic Manuscript Library, (HMML) Collegeville.

H — Hamburg, N. Germany, Staats-und Universitatsbibliothek, MS Petri 51, ff. 6v–7v, XIV, *Anon;* omits the title, inscription and about fifty lines including the epilogue.

L — London, England, British Library, MS Harley 1016, ff. 69r–71r, *Anon*, n.d., microfilmed thanks to the British Library, London.

La — Lambach, Austria/Germany, MS LXXI, ff. 145v, c. 2, 146r, c. 1, XIV, *Anon*, reproduced thanks to Dr Plante and HMML, no. 790; this passage, although in a beautiful hand, is too severely abbreviated to be useful to a collator.

M — Munich, Germany Staatsbibliothek, MS lat. 1287 (Clementinum 14303. Em. D 27) ff. 114–118r, XIII, S. Emmeram, Regensburg, *Anon*, microfilmed thanks to Dr Karl Dachs, Munich.

ON — Oxford, England, Bodleian, New College, MS 140, 72–75r, XIII

exeunte, Anon; ON, as OR and OT, microfilmed thanks to Dr
Bruce Barker-Benfield, The Bodleian Library, Oxford.

OR – Oxford, Bodleian, MS Rawlinson G 38 (14769), 47r–54r, XII *exeunte, Serlo,* see ON above.

OT – Oxford, Bodleian, Trinity College MS 19, ff. 127r–128r, XII *exeunte,* Ste Marie de Radingensi, *A.S.* marg.; see N. R. Ker,
Medieval Libraries, pp. 158, 295; see ON above.[11]

– – Oxford, Corpus Christi College MS 62, ff. 193–196, listed in
Bloomfield, *Incipits* 8936, an error for C above.

P1 – Paris, France, B.N. MS lat. 2590, ff. 49r c, 1, to 50v c. 2, XIII, B.
Hauréau, *Notices et extraits de quelques manuscripts latins de la
Bibliothèque Nationale,* I, 109–125, *Anon,* microfilmed along with
the other Parisian MSS, thanks to the CNRS, Paris.

P2 – Paris, B.N., MS lat. 2795, ff. 116r–124r, XIII, Abbaye de Bon-
port, diocèse d'Evreaux, *Serlo,* Hauréau I, 123–125; *olim* Colbert
5207, Regius 4046[5A]; seen on microfilm thanks to CNRS.

P3 – Paris, B.N. MS lat. 2915, ff. 86v–88v, XIII *ineunte,* Chartreuse de
Bourgfontaine, diocèse de Soissons; f. 22, *Iste liber est fontis Nostre
Domine Cartusiensis ordinis, suessionensis diocesis, ex libris seculi
XVI;* f. 60, Colbert 3639, Regius 4575 (6C). For a MS descrip-
tion I am indebted to Anne-Véronique Gilles and the *Institut de
Recherche et d'Histoire des Textes, section latine,* B.N., Paris; see also
STEPHANUS DE LINGUA TONANTE, by Phyllis Barzillay
Roberts, (Toronto, PIMS, 1968, Studies and Texts 16, p. 161).
See P1 above.

P4 – Paris, France, B.N., MS lat. 15732, ff. 179v, c. 2 to 183r, c. 2,
XII, *Anon;* seen on microfilm, thanks to the CNRS.

P5 – Paris, France, B.N., MS lat. 16878, ff. 157v, c. 1 to 158v, c. 1,
XII, S. Martin, *Serlo;* Hauréau I, 123; microfilmed thanks to
CNRS.

P6 – Paris, France, Bibliothèque Ste-Geneviève MS 1422, ff. 1r–3r,
XIII, Augustins *ecclesie Sti Patri de Villabeata, postea* l'Abbaye de
Ste-Geneviève, *Magister Serlo;* microfilmed thanks to J.
Glenisson of the CNRS.

P7 – Paris, France, B.N. MS lat. 13429, *olim* Bibliothèque St-Germain,
MS 663, *prius ex libris abbatiae Jumièges;* this MS has the title, *Exposito orationis dominice,* followed by forty-nine sermons on the

Pater Noster, of a later date and not attributable to Serlo of Wilton. On the first folio in the hand of Anselme le Michel, however, this MS has a most important note, which indicates that Jumièges once possessed a MS similar to Evreux 41, in attributing an exposition on the *Pater Noster* to Serlo of Wilton: *Exposito orationis dominice. In ueteri catalogo bibliothece huius monasterii* [Jumièges], *inter alios libros unus sic inscribitur: Expositio Serlonis, abbatis de Elemosyna, super Oratione dominica;* Hauréau I 124–25. Surprisingly Jean Carmignac, in *Recherches sur le Notre Père,* (Letouzey & Ane, Paris 1969) p. 164, refers only to this MS, which does not contain the text of Serlo of Wilton: *'avant 1173, Serlon (de Wilton), abbé de l'Aumône, manuscript latin 13429 (folios 69 verso à 86) à la Bibliothèque National de Paris'.*

PE — Peterborough Abbey Library, England MS no. 102, *Tractatus Magistri Serlonis super Orationem Dominicam,* according to M. R. James, *Lists of Manuscripts formerly in the Peterborough Abbey Library,* (Oxford, 1926) p. 45; unfortunately this manuscript is not included in the list of MSS identifiable as coming from the Library of Peterborough Abbey, though the catalogue title is significant; see N. R. Ker, *Medieval Libraries,* pp. 150–52.

R — Rouen, France, Bibliothèque Municipale, MS A 506 (old number A 443) ff. 248r–257r, XII, St-Ouen de Rouen, *Anon,* microfilmed thanks to the Librarian.

S — Salisbury Cathedral, England, MS 97, ff. 68v, c. 1 to 70v, c. 1. XIII, *Serlo,* now in the University Library, Southampton, microfilmed thanks to G. Hampson, the Librarian.

W — Wilhering, Austria, Stiftsbibliothek, MS IX, 138, ff. 139r–139v, XIV, *anon.,* reproduced thanks to Dr Plante and HMML no. 2912; here are three very short excerpts: a) from the intro. with rubric: *deus protegit nos nunc per se, nunc per filium, nunc spiritum sanctum;* b) from the sixth petition with rubric: *de triplici temptatione;* c) from the prologue with rubric: *quomodo pater confortet cor hominis.*

a — 'a' is substituted in the *apparatus criticus,* where the variants of MSS A and M are identical.

d — 'd' is substituted, where variants of MSS D and P4 (XII C) and P1 (XIII C) are identical; these three MSS, all *anon.,* share variant readings plus the suspect lines of the first petition, 90–93: *Illa enim quasi* . . . *insipiens ipse non esset;* all are preceded by the *opusculum magistri Moysi de Grecia: Preterierunt iam plures anni;* D and P4 are followed by the *Comparatio clibani, claustri et uirginali uteri* by Richard of St Victor with the *incipit: Carbonum et cinerum et reliquiis,* which is also included in P1.

g — is substituted, where three MSS of the thirteenth century, B, G and P6 have identical variant readings.

    The following schema relates the MSS by centuries; MSS in parentheses attribute the work to *Serlo,* the others are *anon.*

XII	(OT)	(A)	(C)	D–P4	OR (1200)		(P5)	R			
XIII		(M)	P3	P1	(B G P6)	ON	(E)	(P2)	(S)	L(?)	
XIV	W		AU								
X V					BE						

    The clear and forceful MS OT,[10] is a copy of a briefer version; it lacks many clauses, and ends at line 312 instead of 335. Three variants are significant: at line 141, OT with P3 reads *sterquilinio* for *sterquilino;* at 210–11, OT with MS a, BE, BR, C, E, ON and S, reads: *se ipsum uidere estimantibus,* rather than *se spiritum* . . . ; and at line 235, OT alone reads the delightful *Paulus paulisper pregustauit,* for *Paulus aliquantisper* of all other manuscripts. The punctuation of OT, resembles that of Eton MS 39. This briefer version is left aside here in favor of the lengthier text of all other manuscripts.

Exposicio Magistri Serlonis

    This *Exposicio* is *anon.* in ten MSS: AU, BE, D, L, M, ON, P1, P3, P4, and R; it is ascribed to *Serlo* in at least ten MSS: A, B, C, E, G, OR, P2, P5, P6 and S, to which should be added OT, P7 and PE. No manuscript attributes the work to Serlo of Savigny. Evreux MS 41 and P7 (as Hauréau argued) attribute the work to Serlo, abbot of Aumône, i.e. of Wilton. Several authors note that the title *Magister* in P6 (and apparently in the lost PE, though not in C) favors the authorship of Serlo of Wilton. The argument was presented forcefully in the Bollandists' *Acta Sanctorum* for 20 October, feastday of Blessed Serlo of Savigny, t. 8, pp. 1013–1014 (Brussels, 1853): *vox magister verisimillime ad Serlonem grammaticum pertinet, et certe non ad B. Serlonem abbatem.* According to Professor Öberg, the title *gram(m)aticus* applies to Serlo of Wilton, SERLON DE WILTON, POEMS LATINS, p. 7, with notes 35–36 (Stockholm, 1965). The work is called an *Exposicio* in MSS A, BE, B, E, and P6, which last begins: *Dominica oratio . . . exposita;* or a *sermo* in MSS D and P4, though not in P1, which omits a title; or a *tractatus* in MSS G and PE, according to the catalogue of M. R. James. The most frequent *titulus* is: *Seruis Christi conseruus eorum serlo dominicam orationem,* found in MSS: B, C, OR, P2 and S (which last after *eorum* adds *qui credunt*). AU awkwardly reads *secundum* for *Serlo;* B anticipates the *titulus* with these words: *Exposicio super dominicam orationem.* Other titles are of interest:

BE – *Adhuc alia expositio eiusdem orationis;*

D, P4 – *Sermo do oratione dominica;*

E – *Expositio Serlonis abbatis de elemonsina super orationem dominicam;*

G – *Incipit tractatus Serlonis super orationem dominicam;*

PE – *Tractatus Serlonis super orationem dominicam;*

P6 – *Dominica oratio a magistro serlone exposita;*

S – *Oratio dominica.*

In all MSS except BE, M and OT, the following text is either spelled out or abbreviated: *Protector noster aspice deus et respice in faciem christi* (Ps 83:10). In all MSS except BE and OT, this *incipit* follows the text: *Protector noster deus pater est, qui suos protegit . . .* After the *Protector noster* of this *incipit,* not a single manuscript substitutes for *pater noster* either *dominus iesus* or *iesus christus.* Both these substitutions, however surprisingly, are found in the catalogues: *dominus iesus,* in the catalogue of Bâle, v. 1, p. 198 (repeated in Pits, Leyser, Oudin and Manitius, according to Professor Öberg, *SERLON DE WILTON,* p. 4, and we may add, in Hans Walther, *Initia,* no 14848); likewise, *iesus christus* is found in Bâle, v. 2, p. 126 (repeated by Leland and Tanner, and in Manitius, according to Öberg, *ibid.*). Genially, Professor Öberg consideres this an instance of *citations imprécises.* All MSS except OT and W, have a common *explicit: summum bonum dulcedo cordium iesus, qui est deus benedictus in secula seculorum.*

Of the sermons included here, then, nos. 1) to 3) belong to Serlo of Savigny; 4) which may belong to Serlo of Savigny, but more likely to Serlo of Wilton, has been placed between the certain works of each; 5) to 7) belong to Serlo of Wilton.

NOTES

1. Archdale A. King, *Cîteaux and Her Elder Daughters,* p. 23, (London, Burns and Oates, 1954).
2. Jacqueline Buhot, *Moyen Âge* 44 (1936) pp. 1–21, 104–21, 178–90, 249–72 Léon Guilloreau, *Revue Mabillon* 5 (1909) pp. 326–35; Bennett Hill, *ABR* 31 (1980) pp. 130–152; see also Francis R. Swietek and Terrence M. Deneen, 'The Episcopal Exemption of Savigny, 1112–1184', *Church History,* 52 (1983) pp. 285–298; *idem* 'Pope Lucius II and Savigny', *ASOC* 39 (1983) pp. 3–25 Francis R. Swietek, 'A savigniac Miracle-Story of the Clairvaux Ur-Mariale', *Cîteaux* 34 (1983) pp. 275–83.
3. *Acta sanctorum Octobris,* pp. 1011–15, (Brussels, 1853). André Wilmart, *Revue Mabillon* 12 (1922) pp. 26–38. MSS listed by Wilmart contain 34 pieces in all; this list is reproduced in J. B. Schneyer, *Repertorium,* Serlon de Vaubadon (Savigniacus) O. Cist, pp. 374–5:

C – *Troyes 227,* ff. 117v–132v, from Clairvaux, XII C., contains in order Wilmart (W) nos. 1–30, but then omits W31–34;

V – *Troyes 1171,* ff. 1r–70v, Ourscamp and Clairvaux XII C., contains the 34 pieces in Wilmart but in a different sequence: 1–14, 16–22, 27, 30, 31–34, 15, 23–26, 28–29;

B – *Paris, B.N. 2681A* ff. 108r–196v, perhaps XII C., of unknown origin, discussed by Wilmart;

P – *Paris, B.N. 2594 latin* ff. 11v–12r, contians one sermon of Serlo of Savigny, W18, which is not in question here;

J – *Oxford, Bodleian, Jesus College,* MS 9, f. 12r, col. 2, XIII C. *exeunte,* of unknown origin, contains an additional excerpt.

4. A. C. Friend, 'SERLO OF WILTON, the Early Years', in *Archivum Latinitatis Medii Aevi,* 24 (1953) pp. 85–100 *idem,* 'The Proverbs of Serlo of Wilton', in *Mediaeval Studies* 16 (1954) pp. 179–185, with bibliography pp. 184–185; Jan Öberg, *SERLON DE WILTON, POEMES LATINS,* in *Acta Universitatis Stockholmiensis, Studia Latina Stockholmiensia* 14 (1965), lists sources for the life of Serlo, p. 11–12, note 47, with bibliography, pp. 233–237; *idem,* 'Einige Bermerkungen zu den Gedichten Serlos von Wilton' in *Mittellateinisches Jahrbuch,* 6 (1970) pp. 98–108. Professor Öberg in POEMES LATINS, p. 9, n. 39, referred to a prospectus of *Corpus Christianorum, Continuatio Mediaevalis* to anticipate a new edition of Blessed Serlo's work, to be prepared by the monks of Quarr Abbey, Isle of Wight; Fr. Frederick Hockey, however, in a letter of July 30, 1982, indicates that this edition is not being actively pursued at his monastery.

5. Bertrand Tissier, *Bibliotheca Patrum Cisterciensium* 6:107–130 (Bonnefontaine, 1664). For permission to obtain and use microcopies of MSS: C, V, B, P, I am indebted to the librarians of the *Bibliothèque Nationale,* Paris, and of MS J, I am indebted to librarians of the Bodleian Library and the library of Jesus College, Oxford.

6. Henry O. Coxe, *Catalogus Codicum* MSS. in Collegiis aulisque Oxoniensibus, II, pp. 3–4; on the fly-leaf is written large: *Iebus maria iohannes hec tria mea spes;* then the word *Sum* is followed by three words blotted out, which probably gave the origin or the ownership, followed by: *Schola crucis: Schola lucis.* Of the four sections in the MS, the first contains an *Expositio moralis* of the historical books of the Old Testament; the second an *Expositio moralis* on the Psalter and the books of Solomon. The first section resembles a *florilegium* of favorite spiritual writers of the twelfth-century: Richard and Hugh of St Victor, Bruno and Stephen, Bernard, Aelred, Isaac of Stella, Guerric of Igny, and many others, including Gilbert of Hoyland with three excerpts already published, and Serlo of Savigny to whom three excerpts are attributed.

7. N. R. Kerr, *Medieval Manuscripts in British Libraries,* II Abbotsford-Keele (Oxford:

Notes

Clarendon, 1977) pp. 672–675. for a microfilm of Eton College MS 39, and the opportunity to check it against the original, I am grateful to the Keeper of the College Library and Collections, both to Patrick Strong and to Paul R. Quarrie. For the attribution of these 48 sermons to Gilbert of Hoyland, see E. Mikkers in *Cîteaux* 14 (1963) p. 270.

8. Hans Walther, *Initia carminum ac versuum medii aevi posterioris latinorum* (Gottingen, 959–69) no. 8661 lists 7 mss., which give this hexameter summary of the ten commandments; Morton Bloomfield, *Incipits of Latin Works on the Virtues and Vices, 1100–1500 A.D.* (Cambridge, Mass., 1979) no. 2479, to Walther's list adds: Cambridge, Corpus Christi 136, and Paris, BN lat. 14572 f. 139. I am indebted to Sr Wilma Fitzgerald of the Pontifical Institute of Mediaeval Studies in Toronto, for these and other references.

9. Edward J. L. Scott, *Index to the Sloane Manuscripts in the British Museum*, London, 1904, p. 488, 'Serlo, Abbot of Savigny, Sermons, 13th cent. Lat. 2478, ff. 73, 83, *Membranaceus, in quarto minori*, ff. 109, saec. XIII et XIV'. This incomplete catalogue divides the MS into nine sections, which are reviewed by J. A. Herbert in *Catalogue of Romances in the Department of Manuscripts in the British Museum*, III 512–519, London, 1910. Herbert gives a brief but incomplete description, divided into eleven sections, followed by a more detailed description of the first 47 folios. He lists ff. 64r–69r as section (5), the *Dissuasiones Ualeriani ad Rufinum ne ducat uxorem*, with *incipit: Loqui probibeor et tacere non possum . . .* and *desinit: Set ne borestem scripsisse uidear, uale*, from Walter Map's *De Nugis Curialium, distinctio IV, capp. 3–5*, ed. Thomas Wright for the Camden Society, no. 50, 1950. Sloane ms. 2478, has readings which at several points clarify Wright's edition. Twice in the same work, *Distinctio II, cc. 4–5*, pp. 70–71, Walter Map cites Serlo of Wilton, abbot of Eleemosina, who related two pleasant stories about St Peter, Archbishop of Tarentaise (1141 to 1174): *Retulit mihi magister Serlo a Wiltunia, abbas Eleemosinae . . . Aliud etiam mibi miraculum ipsum in crastina fecisse idem Serlo narravit*. Herbert lists as (6) a single paragraph on f. 70v: *Letter from the Emperor Otho IV to King John urging a reconciliation with the Church*; n.d.: *O. dei gracia Romanorum Rex et sempter Augustus*, and ff. 71r–72v as (7), Letter from St Bernard to the Canons of Lyon (P.L., 182: col. 332), Ep. I, SBOp 7 VII, pp. 388–392.

10. (p. 14) Joseph Goering, 'The Summa de Penitentia of Magister Serlo', in *Mediaeval Studies*, 38 (1976) pp. 1–53, and 40 (1978) pp. 290–311: 'The *Summa de penitentia* of an as yet unidentified *magister* Serlo, which is edited here, was first discussed by L. E. Boyle, who correctly described it as a confessor's manual of English inspiration written sometime after 1234'.

11. Referring to C. De Visch, *Bibliotheca Sacri Ordinis Cisterciensis*, Douai, 1649, Fr. Jean Leclercq, in 'Écrits monastiques sur la Bible aux XIe–XIIIe siècles', *MS* 15 (1953) pp. 102–103, depending on two marginal ascriptions *A.S.*, attributed two sermons in OT to Gilbert of Hoyland, Abbot of Swineshead. Dr C. H. Talbot, however, in *Traditio* 8 (1952) interpreted this *A.S.* as Serlo, Abbot of Savigny. In *Sacris Erudiri* 10 (1958) pp. 192–193, Dom Anselme Hoste described OT as a copy of London, B. M., MS Royal 10 C III, where in the catalogue description, item no. 4, *Quedam exposicio super oracionem dominicam et canonem misse* is from an important treatise of Pope Innocent III, *De sacro altaris mysterio* (Migne, PL 217: cc. 897–906); that work, however, is quite different from the *Expositio* of OT.

OT concludes with forty-three sermons, ff. 122r, c. 1, to 152v, c. 1. The first six sermons, attributed to *A.C.*, are printed in the words of Bernard, Abbot of Clairvaux. The last thirty-four sermons, attributed in the margins to *A.R.* (Abbot or Aelred of Rievaulx), should be collated with Aelred's sermons published by Bernard Tessier (Migne, vv. 184 and 195) and others by C. H. Talbot, *Sermones inediti B. Aelredi abbatis Rievalensis* (Rome: Curia Generalis S.O.C., 1952) and with two newly noted MSS: Paris, B.N. new acquisitions, lat. 294, and Troyes B.M. 868; see Gaetano Raciti, in *Coll.* 45 (1983) pp. 166–178, and Brian Patrick McGuire, in *The Downside Review*, 103 (1985) pp. 147–150.

Of the three intervening pieces the first, *Oratio dominica* correctly, but the second *Seraphim* incorrectly, are ascribed in the margins to *A.S.*, while the third, *Ibimus uiam trium dierum*, in this ms. remains anonymous. This third piece resembles the *De tribus dietis* of Robert of Sorbonne, printed by Felix Chambron (Paris, 1902) p. xvii, according to the editors of *Incipits of Latin Works on the Virtues and Vices*, 2474, 6414, 6415, (Mediaeval Academy of America, Cambridge, 1979), where the editors refer to Glorieux, 159, 1. The second piece, ascribed to A.S., *Seraphim stabant super illud*, is from a work of Alan of L'Isle (Migne, P.L. 210, cc. 172–180); see also *Incipits*, 0214, 4054, 4055. The first piece, on the *Pater Noster*, attributed to A.S., is a copy of a briefer version of Abbot Serlo's explanation of the *Pater*, but lacks both title and introduction. Apparently in the same hand, OT has neat marginal summaries resembling those of ON, another Bodleian ms., but much briefer than those of S, now in Southampton University Library. These notes of ON, OT and S, are here printed immediately below Serlo's text.

    These sermons in OT, belong to the last part of the twelfth century (N. R. Ker, *Medieval Libraries of Great Britain, a list of surviving books*, 2nd ed. p. 158, (London: Offices of the Royal Historical Society, 1964). The ms was the gift of Radulphus de Dymmoc, formerly prior of Reading Abbey (Ker, p. 295); see also H. O. Coxe, *Catalogus codicum MSS. qui in collegiis aulisque Oxoniensibus hodie adseruantur* vol. II, Oxford: 1852, Trinity College section pp. 9–10).

    12. John L. McKenzie, *Dictionary of the Bible* (MacMillan, N.Y. 1965) 'Apocalypse;' William G. Heidt, OSB, *The book of the Apocalypse* (Collegeville: Liturgical Press, 1962) pp. 80–81; T. F. Glasson '*The Revelation of John*,' (Cambridge: University Press, 1965) pp. 66–67; John Randall, *The Book of Revelation: what does it really say?* (Locust Valley: Living Flame Press, 1976); J. Massyngberde Ford, *Revelation* in *The Anchor Bible* (Garden City, NY: Doubleday, 1975); André Feuillet, *The Apocalypse*, trans. Thos. E. Crane (Staten Island, NY: Alba House, 1964) refers to Jean Mariana, *Scholia in Vetus et Novum Testamentum* (Madrid, 1619; Paris, 1620; Antwerp, 1624); M. E. Boismard, *l'Apocalypse* (4th ed. Paris: Cerf, 1972); J. Munk, *Petruc und Johannes in der Offenbarung Johanni* (Copenhagen, 1950). Paul S. Minear, 'Ontology and Ecclesiology in the Apocalyse,' in *New Testament Studies* 13 (1968) p. 96. Cornelii à Lapide, *Commentaria in Scripturam Sacram* (Paris: Vivès, 1860) XIV, c. 399; Ronald A. Knox, *A New Testament Commentary For English Readers* (London: Burns Oates, 1958); Austin Farrer, *A Rebirth of Images, The Making of St John's Apocalypse*, (Westminster: Dacre Press, 1949) pp. 127–135.

    13. *Cerimoniale*, 'is used here as an alternative to *figurativum*. . . . What he means, I think, is "allegorical," in the sense that all the liturgical prescriptions of the Mosaic Law were thought to have allegorical meanings for Christians. The idea goes back to the Epistle of Barnabas, which maintained that the Jews had misinterpreted all the Mosaic cultic legislation, by taking it literally. *Figurativa* then equals "typical" sense: the Jewish sabbath was a type of the Christian Sunday. But Serlo's point seems to be that the sense has changed. Originally the word (he would think of *sabbatum*) did mean sabbath literally, and Sunday typically. But when the Church arrived and made Sunday its holy day, then the literal meaning of the commandment changed from Saturday to Sunday. I think Serlo is concerned to show that the one consistent literal meaning is: "keep holy the day of rest, and the specification of the latter is something secondary, not of the esence of the commandment.'" For this clarification I am grateful to Fr R. A. F. MacKenzie, Regis College.

    13. The section of *incipits* of Latin works on the *Pater Noster*, in *Incipits of Latin Works*, ed. by Morton W. Bloomfield *et al.*, indicates the frequency of commentaries on the *Pater* between 1100 and 1500; entries run from 8001 to 9261. pp. 567–686. For a short bibliography of modern commentaries see Raymond E. Brown 'The Pater Noster as an eschatological Prayer' in *New Testament Essays* (3rd ed., New York, Paulist Press, 1965).

    14. *uiri secundum deum sensati*, possibly from Sirach 6:36, *si uideris sensatum euigila ad illum*, or from Sirach 26:26; see R. A. F. MacKenzie, *Sirach*, (Wilmington: Glazier, 1983) pp. 45, 107. To an author with the pseudonym *Sensatus* were attributed *Sermones Spirituales*; see Thomas Ittig, *De Bibliothecis et catenis patrum variisque ueterum scriptorum ecclesiasticorum collecionibus*, (Leipsic 1707, reprint, Ridgewood, NJ: Gregg, 1965) p. 550, where Ittig regrets their loss: *Par fortuna sermonum spiritualium Sensati*; see *Sensati sermones spirituales*, Alberti Fabricii, *Bibliotheca Latina Mediae et Infimae aetatis*, 6:456 (reprint Graz,

1962), and "Sensatus" (Antonius Penter, Collector: Wien, Nat. 3897) Clm *(Isti sermones de epistolis de tempore a sermonibus Guidonis d'Evreux dependent)*:J.-B. Schneyer, *Repertorium Sermonum*, Bd. V, under *Sensatus*, pp. 358–374; but an author dependent on Guido of Evreux (OP, fl. c. 1290–93), is too late for the *Sensatus* of this passage.

PETER AND PAUL,
TWO OLIVE TREES

For the feast of Peter and Paul, June 29, Serlo chooses a text from the 'symbolic-allegorical vision' of the Apocalypse (11:4–7). This text, now read on Saturdays for the 33rd week in ordinary time, in the new lectionary has the rubric: 'these two prophets have been a plague to the peoples of the earth'. In Zechariah (4:3 and 4:14) the two olive trees and the two anointed are considered to be Joshua and Zerubbabel, Jewish priestly and civic leaders; the oil and the light of their leadership, Serlo applies to Peter and Paul. In the Apocalypse (11:4) the two olive trees and lamps with allusion to Joshua and Zerubbabel, seem to be Peter and Paul. In Apocalypse 11:5–6 the two avengers have the attributes of Elijah and Moses, which Serlo applies to Peter and Paul. The crisis for which the book was written, 'must be the early persecutions by Roman authorities. . . . Babylon is Rome, the city of the seven hills (17:5, 9). The number of the beast, 666 (13:8), represents the sum of the numerical value of the letters of the name Caesar Nero written in Hebrew characters (KSR NRWN)', writes John L. McKenzie. André Feuillet finds that to equate the witnesses with Peter and Paul, 'is to face the insurmountable difficulties', which he proceeds to enumerate. Paul S. Minear believes 'it is impossible to limit the identity of the two olive trees to two specific prohets'. Cornelius à Lapide says the allegorical interpretation suggests primarily Christ and his Church but secondarily Peter and Paul. Ronald Knox remarks that the 'witnesses, whether you think of them as Zorobabel and Josue in Zacharias' prophecy, or as Moses and Elias in Jewish apocalyptic, or as Peter and Paul in recent history, symbolize the ever resurgent protest of the Church.[1][2]

I. WILMART 15
B, ff. 131v–134v; C, ff. 122r, c. 2 to 122v, c.2; V, ff. 50r–52v.

Rubric: Item eiusdem in natale apostolorum petri et pauli
Isti sunt due olive et duo candelabra, stantes in conspectu
domini terre: et si quis eos nocere uoluerit ignis exiet de ore
ipsorum, et deuorabit inimicos eorum. Et si quis uoluerit eos
5 *ledere: sic oportebit eum occidi. Hi enim habent potestatem*
claudere celum, ne pluat diebus prophetie ipsorum: et potestatem
habent super aquas conuertendi eas in sanguinem, et percutere terram
omni plaga quotienscumque uoluerint: et cum finierint testimonium
suum: bestia que ascendet de abysso: faciet aduersus eos bellum:
10 *et uincet eos et occidet* (Apoc 11:4–7).
   Quanti meriti fuerint isti sancti: patet ex auctoritate scripture
ubi dicitur: *isti sunt due oliue.* Oliua est arbor plena succo:
et isti pleni fuerunt spiritu sancto: qui per oliuam significatur.
Hac enim unctione infusi que docet de omnibus: alios docuerunt, et
15 *lumen uere claritatis in mundo sparserunt: et sanauerunt dolores*
uitiorum. Unde dicuntur candelabra lucencia ante dominum. Placita
enim sunt eorum uita et doctrina: *et si quis uoluerit eis nocere:*
ignis (f. 132r) *exiet de ore ipsorum*, etc. Hic est ignis diuini
verbi de quo dictum est: *ignitum eloquium tuum uehementer.*
20 *Qui deuorat inimicos*: quia causa est dampnationis eorum. Unde
dominus in euangelio. *Si quis uos non receperit: excutite puluerem*
pedibus uestris super eos in testimonium (Lc 9:5). Puluis signum
est laboris uie. Hic excutitur super non recipientes quia labor
predicatorum causa erit dampnationis malorum.
25   *Habent potestatem claudere celum nubibus*, etc. Huius rei figura
precessit in helia (3 R 7:1–6, 18:41–45): qui oratione clausit
et aperuit celum. Quod sancti modo spiritaliter adimplent. *Celum*
enim scriptura sacra intelligitur: que et celat diuina secreta et
calorem caritatis administrat: et uirtutibus pollet, ut *celum* stellis.
30 Legitur deus *celum*, id est, firmamentum fecisse inter aquas
superiores et inferiores: hoc est, inter angelos et homines (Gen 1:
6–7). Angeli scilicet aque superiores ad uidendum deum et cogno-

---

1. BV om. titulum. 5. B eos. 7. B conuerti (at linea 57, B convertendi). 14. V alii. 16.
HCV lucentia. 22. C pedum uestrorum. 23. V respicientes. 25. BV om. nubibus. 29. B
charitatis amministrat, V aministrat.

Two Olive Trees

'These witnesses are the two olive trees and the two lampstands standing in the presence of the Lord of the earth. If anyone tries to harm them, fire will burst from their lips to devour their enemies. In this way whoever tries to harm them will be slain. They have authority to close up the sky, so that during the time of their mission there will be no rainfall. They have authority over the waters also, to turn them into blood and at will to strike the earth with plagues of every kind' (Rev 11:4–7).

How deserving were these saints is evident from the authority of scripture, which says 'they are the two olive trees.' An olive tree is full of oil; they were filled with the holy Spirit, symbolized by the olive. Steeped in this unction, which teaches all things, they have taught others, have shed upon the world a light of real brilliance and healed the wounds inflicted by the vices. Hence they are called the lampstands luminous before the Lord, because their lives and teaching were gratifying. 'If anyone tries to harm them, fire will burst from their lips.' This is the fire of the divine word of whom it was said: 'your eloquence is a raging fire (Ps 118:140),' which swallows your enemies, because it effects their damnation. Hence the Lord says in Luke (9:15): 'if anyone does not welcome you, shake the dust off your feet over them as a warning.' Dust is a sign of toil on the road. It is shaken off upon those who refuse a welcome, because the toil of preachers will effect the condemnation of the wicked. 'They have authority to close the sky' with clouds, etc. This was illustrated in Elijah (3 K 17:1–6; 18:41–45). With prayer, he closed and opened heaven. This the saints now accomplish spiritually, since heaven means the holy scripture, which conceals divine mysteries, provides the warmth of charity and is filled with virtues as the heavens with stars. We read that God established heaven, that is, the firmament, between the waters above and below, that is, between angels and men (Gen 1:6–7). The angels, of course, as the waters above, do not need aid from the scriptures to see

scendum, non egent amminiculo scripturarum: et ideo dicuntur esse
super firmamentum. Homines uero per celum ascendunt ad deum: quia
35 per scripturas in cognitione dei proficiunt. Hoc *celum* sancti claudunt,
quando scripturas clausas retinent, ne dent *sanctum canibus*,
aut spargant *margaritas* inter *porcos* (Mt 7:6 f. 132u). Aliis uero
scilicet obedientibus aperiunt, ut in eis erudiantur et fructum
faciant.
40   Unde dominus ait. *Uobis datum est nosse mysterium regni dei*
(Lc 8:10), id est, sacramentum scripturarum: *ceteris autem in parabolis,*
ut uidentes non uideant: et audientes non intelligant. Ideo
in parabolis audiunt scripturas: quia mali, meritis suis exigentibus,
excecati sunt. He sunt *palpebre* domini, que *interrogant*, id
45 est, probant *filios hominum* (Ps 10:5). *Palpebre* que aperiuntur et
clauduntur: significant apertiones et opertiones scripturarum.
Palpebre aperte interrogant bonos et malos: quia boni et humiliter
intelligunt et operantur, et non sibi sed domino ascribunt. Mali
uero negligunt operari: et a se non a domino se habere scientiam
50 reputant. Item scripture clause similiter et bonos et malos interrogant:
quia boni pie ignorant: mali despiciunt, et corrumpunt.
    Unde in psalmo. *Intonuit de celo dominus. Intonuit*
minis: *dedit uocem* blandiendo in promissis *de celo*: hoc est, per
predicatores. Et ecce *grando et carbones ignis*: hoc est predicatores
55 aliis facti sunt *grando* contundentes et redarguentes malos.
    Alios uero igne caritatis (f. 133r) accensos, *carbones* ignitos reddiderunt:
et habent potestatem super aquas conuertendi eas in sanguinem.
Hic per *aquas*: scientia diuina accipitur. Hec conuertitur
in sanguinem: hoc est in peccatum reprobis et contemptoribus. Cum
60 enim boni in diuina proficiunt sapientia per fidem et obedientiam:
mali quia contemnunt, deteriores fiunt. Hoc significatum est, in
moyse, qui *conuertit aquas in sanguinem*, ne egyptii biberent (Ex 7:17):
et percutere omni plaga, quod in plagis egypti figuratur (Ex
7-11). *Quotiescunque uoluerint*, id est, tempore congruo.
65   Diligenter perpendendum, si uideremus homines talia facere,
ignem emittere ad deuorationem inimicorum: *celum claudere, conuertere*

---

36. V quoniam. 38. V exaudiantur. 41. V inv. scripturarum sacramentum. 43. C malis.
44. BV Hec. 45. V inv. filios hominum probant. 46. B operciones. 63. B omini. 64. B
quotiensque.

and know God. Therefore they are said to be above the firmament. But men rise to God through the heavens, because through scripture they advance in the knowlege of God. Saints close this heaven, when they keep the scriptures closed, lest (132v, c. 1) they toss to dogs what is holy or set pearls before swine (Mt 7:6). But to others who obey, they disclose the scriptures, that they may be schooled in scripture and produce fruit.

Hence, the Lord said: 'knowledge of the secrets of the kingdom of God,' that is, the sacrament of the scriptures, 'has been given to you but to the rest it comes through parables, that looking they may not see and listening they may not understand (Lk 8:10).' Therefore in parables they hear the scriptures, because as their own demerits demand they have been blinded. These eyelids belong to the Lord, for they scrutinize, or test the children of men (Ps 10:5). Eyelids which are opened and closed, mean the opening and closing of scripture. The open eyelids of God question the good and the wicked, because the good understand and act humbly and pay tribute not to themselves but to the Lord. The wicked fail to act and claim they have knowledge through themselves and not from God. The closed scriptures question the good and the wicked alike, because the good are devoutly ignorant of them and the wicked despise and corrupt them.

Consequently 'the Lord thundered in the sky' (Ps 18:13). He 'thundered' with threats and 'spoke aloud,' wooing with promises, 'from heaven,' that is, through preachers. Behold 'the hailstones and flashes of fire' (Ps 18:12). This means that for some the preachers became 'hailstones,' to strike and rebuke the wicked, but they set others alight like 'embers,' burning in the fire of charity. 'They have power over the waters to turn them into blood.' By 'waters' here is meant divine wisdom. This wisdom 'is turned into blood,' that is, into sin for the condemned and the scoffers. Indeed, while through faith and obedience the good advance in divine wisdom, the wicked grow worse, because they are scoffers. This was illustrated in Moses, who 'changed water into blood,' lest the Egyptians quench their thirst (Ex 7:17). They 'struck the earth with every plague' (Ex 7:11), which is illustrated in the plagues of Egypt. 'At will,' that is, on fitting occasions.

This should be carefully weighed. If we were to see people doing such deeds: 'casting flames' to devour enemies, 'shutting the heavens, turning

aquas in sanguinem, eos uere ultra homines estimaremus: et ut spiritales
mirabiliter ueneraremur. Si uero uideremus eosdem a bestia deuoratos: eos
miseros et miserabiles iudicaremus. Quod et factum
70   est. Sequitur. *Bestia que ascendit ab abysso:* etc. *Bestia* ista
intelligitur collectio malorum, bestialiter uiuentium: ab initio
mundi usque ad finem. Cuius caput est diabolus: et principale
membrum antichristus. De quo alibi dicitur (f. 133v). *Bestia erat*
similis pardo: pedes eius sicut ursi: os eius sicut os leonis (Apoc 13:2).
75   *Pardus* maculosum animal significat uarietatem: quam illi
habent in heresibus suis. *Pedes ursi:* quia diuina sacramenta conculcant.
Os leonis cuius dentes naturaliter secent: quia uerba
fetida et alios corrumpentia emittunt. Hec bestia *ascendit de*
abysso: id est, per tenebrosos manifestabit potentiam, et obtinebit
80   regnum.
      Hec *bestia* aperte se demonstrauit in persecutione martyrum.
Quia uero ex eorum morte miraculis crebrescentibus ex fide etiam
persecutorum sancta ecclesia proficiendo creuit, et hostis impetuosa
tribulatio non profuit: idea conuertit se ad aliud, et immisit
85   hereticos, qui scripturas sacras peruerterent: et simplices sub
obtentu religionis deciperent.

Sic *bestia* assumpsit pellem ouinam:
ut tegeret intus rabiem lupinam.

Contra quod doctores sancti diuino nutu excitati: hereticam praui-
90   tatem confutauerunt: et ueritatem fidei lucidius manifestauerunt.
      Unde propheta ad dominum. *Increpa* domine *feras harundinis;*
increpa, conuince *feras,* hereti−(f. 134r)−cos bestialiter
uiuentes: quia sicut harundo exterius est nitida et interius
uacua, et crescit in paludibus; sic heretici exterius proferunt
95   nitorem eloquentie, intus uacui a ueritate: et in paludibus crescunt,

---

87-8 similiter desinens, cujus auctorem non inveni. 96 *ieronimus,* quem Serlo hic non
verbatim sed secundum sensum saepius citat, e.g. de castitate vel luxurie, PL 24:136A,
728C; 25:324D; cf. perplures ad haereticos allusiones, quas in ejus operum indice videri
libet, PL 30:987−88.

---

71. C inicio. 79. B abisso; potenciam. 82. V crescentibus. 83. B profitiendo. 85. C corrumperent. 90. V lucidis.

streams into blood,' we would really consider them supermen, and would reverence them with awe as men of spirit. But if we were to see the same people devoured by a beast, we would consider them pitiful and pitiable. But this is what follows: 'a beast rose from the abyss.' This beast means the crowd of the wicked living like beasts from the beginning to the end of the world. The devil is their head and antichrist is their leader. Later this holy book says: 'the beast was like a leopard, a spotted animal with the paws of a bear and the jaws of a lion' (Apoc 13:12). 'The leopard,' a spotted animal, means the variety they display in their heresies; 'a bear's paws,' because they trample on the divine mysteries; 'a lion's teeth,' because they have a natural cutting edge, because they utter words which are rank and infect others. This beast 'rises from the abyss,' that is, /will show its power through the darkness and seize the kingdom.

This 'beast' displayed itself openly in persecuting the martyrs. But thanks to their deaths, increased by the miraculous conversion even of their persecutors, the church continued to grow and the rabid provocations of the foe did not prevail. Hence the enemy, adopting a different strategy, dispatched heretics to tamper with the scripture and cozen the simple under the pretext of piety. So the beast donned sheepskin to disguise the wolfish fury within. Against this dodge, aroused by divine inspiration, holy doctors refuted the heretical distortions and revealed the truth through the illuminations of faith.

Hence the prophet pleads with the Lord: 'O Lord, strike the wild beasts of the swamp' (Ps 67:31). 'Strike,' confound 'the wild beasts,' the heretics who live like beasts. As a reed shines outside and is hollow within and grows in swamps, so heretics show the glitter of eloquence without, but are devoid of truth within, and grow in marshes, that is,

id est, demorantur in luto luxurie. Sicut qit beatus ieronimus.
Uix uidebis hereticum castum; et necesse est ut increpes quia
congregatio taurorum, id est, heresiarcharum est, in *uaccis populorum*,
id est, in seductilibus populis (Ps 67:31). Sed non proficiunt,
100 dei gratia adiuuante, quia potius ad hoc sunt, ut excludantur,
etc.: id est, ut per eos illi qui probati sunt in diuinis eloquiis
manifesti fiant. Magistri tauri: populi uacce. Diabolus autem
confusus in hac parte: non tamen quieuit: potius immisit falsos
fratres: qui bonis familiariter adherendo subtilius eos corrumperent.
105 Et quia in his maxime inualuit inimicus: propterea plangit
ecclesia in iheremia dicens. *Uelociores fuerunt* inimici nostri
aquilis celi; in montibus persecuti sunt nos: in deserto insidiati
nobis (Lam 4:19). Hoc est, magis nocuerunt maligni spiritus perse-
quendo: quam profuerunt boni angeli adiuuando. *In montibus perse-*
110 *(f. 134 v) -cuti sunt nos*: quia prelatos obtinuerunt. *In deserto*
insidiati sunt nobis: quia usque ad religiosos claustrales, falsorum
fratrum adiutorio peruenerunt.
          Habet hec bestia capita .vii.: et cornua .x. (Apoc 12:3) Per
capita .vii. principalia uitia: Per *cornua* persecutores ecclesie
115 ad destruenda .x. precepta legis. In huius rei figura antichristo
.x. reges adherebunt, per quos ipse et ecclesiam impugnabit, et
mundum sibi subiugabit. Huius bestie membrum fuit nero, qui petrum
et paulum hodie occidit corporaliter: sed ipse occisus est spiritualiter.
Ecce *ignis* qui exiuit *de ore eorum* ad deuorandum inimicum
120 eorum neronem. Isti sunt nobis exemplum, ut in bonis operibus non
superbiamus: et horribilem mortem pro domino non timeamus.

---

100. B adiuuantes. 103. C in hac parte confusus. 105. C quia add. enim. 106. CV
ieremia. 113. CV decem. 115. C decem. 119-20 C inv. neronem inimicum eorum.

dwell in the mire of luxury. As Jerome says. 'Rarely will you find a chaste heretic.' You must confound them 'because a convention of bulls,' that is, of heresiarchs mingles with 'the herds of the peoples' that is, with those easily led. But thanks to the grace of God, they are making no headway. Rather, they are on the verge of being evicted. Thanks to them, men tried and true in preaching are becoming recognized. The masters are bulls; the people a herd of cows. The devil, however, though foiled on this front, has not relaxed. Rather, he has inserted false brethren, who by intermingling in a familiar way, are to corrupt the good. Because the foe has made great inroads, the church laments with Jeremiah (Lam 4:19): 'our enemies, swifter than eagles, swooped from the sky. They tracked us down on the hills; they took us by surprise in the desert.' This means that malicious spirits harmed us more by persecution than the good angels suceeded in helping us. 'They tracked us down on the hills,' by winning over our prelates. 'They took us by surprise in the desert,' because through the help of false brethren, they penetrated even into religious cloisters.

'This beast has seven heads and ten horns' (Rev 12:3). The 'seven heads' are the capital sins. The 'horns' are the persecutors of the church, who destroy the ten precepts of the law. As an illustration, ten kings cling to antichrist, through whom he will attack the church and subject the world to himself. One member of this beast was Nero, who on this day slew Peter and Paul in the body, only to be slain himself in the spirit. See, there is the 'fire,' which came 'from their mouths' to devour Nero, their enemy. They are an example for us, that we should neither brag of our good works nor fear a horrible death for the Lord.

II. WILMART 26 COMMANDMENTS AND PLAGUES

In a sermon to the people of Rheims, Serlo comments on the two musical instruments of praise: the cithara or lyre and the psaltery or harp. 'The lyre, which plays bass notes, means mortification of the flesh and in earthly things sobriety of life. The harp, which plays higher notes, means the contemplation and love of heavenly life.'

With St Augustine, Serlo compares the ten commandments to the ten-stringed harp, and with St Isidore he compares those who violate the commandments to the Egyptians who suffered the ten plagues. The three commandments on the first tablet refer to the love of God and the seven on the second tablet refer to the service of our neighbor. These ten are summed up in love for God and for one's neighbor.

Because the Egyptians despised God's commands they were visited with the ten plagues, each plague apposite for the commandment violated. For example, the punishment for violating the fourth commandment is the dog-fly, and here Serlo sums up in a riming couplet, the author of which I have not discovered:

> unde: qui parentes non ueneratur,
> merito pena canum multatur.

> hence: if your parents you will slight,
> you shall feel the gadfly bite.

Finally each commandment is neatly summed up in one or two words. The order of the fifth and sixth commandments is reversed, both in Serlo and in Augustine:

> Quintum, allidit fornicationem, Sexum, crudelitatem.

The fifth destroys fornication, the sixth cruelty.

B, 164r–167v; C, 129r, c. 2 – 129v, c. 2; V, 61v–64v.

Rubric: Item eiusdem habitus remis ad populum
*Confitemini domino in cithara, in pasalterio decem cordarum psallite
illi* (Ps 32:2) . Nos congregati ut deo seruiamus: in duobus maxime
eum laudare debemus: scilicet in dispositione temporalium et carnis
5　mortificatione; et in contemplatione celestium et desiderio celestis
uite. Per citharam namque que ab inferioribus resonat mortificatio
carnis et sobrietas uite in terrenis designatur. (164v) Per
psalterium quod a superioribus sonat, contemplatio et amor uite
celestis significatur. Hoc decem cordas habere dicitur, quia decem
10　sunt precepta que de celestibus nobis data sunt. In his debemus
deo psallere et ipsa adimplendo precepta ipsum magnificare nobis
utile est.

Decem autem preceptorum tria fuerunt in una tabula; que sunt
de dilectione dei: septem in alia, que pertinent ad utilitatem
15　proximi. Primum mandatum est: *audi israel. Deus tuus deus unus est*
(Deut 6:4). Quia enim populi stulticia in errorem ydolatrie miserabiliter
corruerat, et multa simulacra uane et supersticiose colebat,
reuocanda erat ad fidem unius dei: et ad cultum et ad dilectionem
ipsius. Propterea dicit: *audi* et cetera, quasi noli culturam
20　falsorum deorum sequi. Unus est enim deus creator et redemptor: et
etiam iudex futurus. Hunc cole solum postpositis ceteris, ut omnium
creaturarum effectorem; ueritatis doctorem: beatitudinis eterne
largitorem.

Sed quia posset homo deum unum colere, et tamen crederet eum
25　creaturam non creatorem; temporalem non eternum: ideo addit secundum preceptum, *non accipies in uanum nomen dei tui*: hoc est eum
quem colis unum deum: ne accipias in uanitate: sed credas creatorem
(165r) non creaturam.

Et enim uanitas est omnis creatura. Et quia posset homo unum
30　deum colere, et creatorem credere; et tamen inde nichil utilitatis

---

2ff. Ut S. Augustinus (PL 38:67, 75a, 75b), ita Serlo psalterio .X. precepta comparat; ut S.
Isidorus (glossa ordinaria, PL 114:254C, 458CD), Serlo eos comparat qui .X. precepta con-
temnant, Egyptiis qui .X. plagis percussi sunt. 73 and 83, quos auctores citet, nescio.

---

1. BV om. titulum. 2. B cythera. 6. CV uite celestis. 9–10. B .x. 14 BV .vii. 30. CV inde
nichil utilitatis.

II. WILMART 26 (B) COMMANDMENTS AND PLAGUES

A Sermon By The Same Author Delivered to the People of Rheims

'Give thanks to the Lord on the lyre; sing him psalms on the ten-stringed harp (Ps 33:2)' We have gathered to serve the Lord. We ought to praise him, in two special ways: first, in managing temporal affairs and in mortifying our flesh, and again in contemplating heavenly affairs and in the desire for heavenly life. The lyre, which plays bass notes, means mortification of the flesh and sobriety of life in earthly things. The harp, which plays higher notes, means the contemplation and love of heavenly life. The harp is said to have ten strings, since ten commandments were given about the concerns of heaven. On these strings, we should sing psalms to the Lord, and by observing his commandments it is to our profit to proclaim how great is the Lord.

Of the ten commandments, three engraved on one tablet, concern the love of God, and seven on the other, concern the profit of our neighbor. This is the first commandment: 'Listen, Israel. Your God is one God (Deut 6:4).' Because in their folly the people pitifully lapsed into the error of idolatry, because in vain superstition they began to worship many idols, they had to be restored to faith in one God and to his worship and love. Therefore he said: 'listen' and so forth, meaning do not follow the worship of false gods. There is indeed one God, our Creator, Redeemer and future Judge. Disregarding others, worship him alone as the Maker of all creatures, the Teacher of truth, and the Giver of eternal happiness.

Because we can worship one God but still believe him a creature and not the Creator, temporal and not eternal, he adds a second precept: 'you shall not take the name of God in vain.' This means that the one you worship as the only God, you may not name in vain, but believe that he is not a creature but the Creator.

Every creature is really vanity. Since we can worship one God and believe him the Creator, but derive no profit, he adds a third command-

assequeretur: addit tertium. *Obserua diem sabbati,* quasi dicat. Ab
eo quem credis unum et colis ut creatorem deum: debes expectare
quietem et eternam felicitatem. In huius rei signo preceptum est
obseruari sabbatum post sex dies, quia post laborem huius uite
35 temporalis perueniemus ad requiem eterne felicitatis. Hec sunt tria
precepta de dilectione dei, ut unum ueneremur; creatorem
agnoscamus: et in eo ueram quietem expectemus.

Septem precepta que in alia tabula continentur, pertinent ad
dilectionem proximi; quia in cursu uite temporalis que septem diebus
40 agitur, debemus exhibere proximo quod nobis fieri uolumus: et
non facere ei quod nobis nolumus fieri. Unde primum preceptum est.
Honora patrem tuum etc.: quia uolumus in senectute honorari a
filiis nostris. Secundum *non mechaberis*: quia nolumus uxores
nostras mechari. Tertium *non occides.* Nolumus enim ab aliis occidi.
45 Quartum *non furaberis*, quia nolumus res nostras ab aliis furari.
Quintum *non falsum testimonium dices*, quia nolumus contra nos falsum
testimonium proferri. Sextum *non concupisces uxorem* (165v)
proximi tui. Nolumus hoc nobis fieri. Septimum *non concupisces*
aliquem rem proximi tui, quia nolumus nobis res nostras auferri.
50 Et est summa istorum mandatorum *diligere deum ex toto corde,*
ex tota anima, ex tota mente, et proximum sicut seipsum (Mt 22:37;
Deut 6:5), et non faciamus ei quod nobis fieri nolumus: et eidem
subueniamus, sicut nobis subueniri uolumus in nostra necessitate.

Hec precepta quia contempserunt egyptii: .x. plagis percussi
55 sunt. Prima enim plaga, *aqua conuersa in sanguinem* (Ex 7:14–25).
Aquam accipe quasi unum deum, ex quo sunt omnia: sicut ex aqua
generantur uniuersa. Hec conuertitur *in sanguinem,* id est, in peccatum, ut bibere non possint ex ea: qui nolunt credere unitatem dei-
tatis. *Aqua* ergo *in sanguinem* conuertitur, quia sensus egyptiorum
60 peccatorum sanguine fedatur: et iusto dei iudicio, factum est ut de
illo fluuio sanguinem biberent: in quo hebreorum pueros necare
consueuerant.

Secunda plaga: *rane* (Ex 8:14–18). Hec significat garrulam
loquacitatem poetarum et sapientium huius seculi, qui non creatorem

---

36. CV cognoscamus. 37. V requiem. 38. BV .vii. 45–47. BV inv. Quartum . . . Quintum . . . 52. B inv. fieri nolumus. 54. C egiptii. 59. C egiptiorum. 64. CV mundi. 65. B
coluere uoluerunt.

ment: 'observe the sabbath day.' From God whom you believe to be one God and worship as Creator, you ought to expect rest and eternal happiness. As a sign of this, it was commanded that after six days the sabbath be observed, because after the toil of this temporal life, we shall reach the peace of eternal happiness. These three commandments concern the love of God: to worship him only, to recognize him as the Creator, and to expect true rest in him.

The seven commandments inscribed on the second tablet, concern the love of our neighbor. In the course of our temporal life, which passes in seven days, we ought to treat our neighbor, as we would like to be treated, and not do to him, what we would not like done to ourselves. Hence the first commandment is: 'honor your father and so forth,' because in old age we wish to be honored by our children. The second: 'do not commit adultery,' because we do not want our spouses to commit adultery. The third: 'do not kill,' because we do not wish to be killed by others. The fourth: 'do not steal,' because we do not wish our goods to be stolen by others. The fifth: 'do not give false witness,' because we do not wish false witness brought against us. The sixth: 'you shall not desire your neighbor's spouse.' We do not want this to happen to us. The seventh: 'do not desire any other possession of your neighbor,' because we do not want our possessions taken from us.

Here is a summary of these commandments: 'love the Lord with all your heart, with all your soul and with all your mind, and your neighbor as yourself' (Mt 22:37). Let us not do to him, what we do not want done to ourselves. Let us help him, as we wish to be helped in our need.

Because they despised these commandments the Egyptians were afflicted with the ten plagues. In the first, 'water was changed into blood' (Ex 7:14–25). By 'water,' understand the one God, from whom all things exist, just as from water the universe is begotten. 'Water is changed into blood,' that is, into sin, that they who refuse to believe in the unity of Godhead, may not drink from it. Water is therefore turned into blood, because the understanding of the Egyptians was muddled by the blood of sins; and by the just sentence of God it happened that they drank blood from that stream, because in it they were wont to drown the Hebrew children.

The second plague was 'the frogs' (Ex 8:14–18). These mean the glib prattle of the poets and philosophers of this world, who were unwilling

65 deum colere uoluerunt. Sed pro creatore creaturas uenerando, quod
dei est: creature attribuerunt. Qui enim christiane (166r) ueritati
contradicunt; et in sua uanitate decepti, decipiunt: *rane* sunt,
tedium afferentes auribus, non cibum mentibus.
Contra diem sabbati *cinifes* ponuntur (Ex 8:16–19): musce in-
70 quiete que nunquam quiescunt. He sunt cure insolentes, et pessime
exagitationes, quibus exagitantur, qui in deo quiescere nesciunt.
Qui enim inquieti sunt, resiliunt a spiritu sancto: et iugiter terrenis
actibus implicantur. De quibus scriptum est. Impedimenta huius mundi
fecerunt eos miseros, et sabbatum, id est, requiem habere
75 non possunt. Contra istorum inquietudinem, debent habere iusti
sabbatum in corde: et sanctificationem spiritus sancti. *Cinifes*
autem musce sunt minutissime, inquietissime; inordinate uolantes:
non permittentes homines quiescere. Dum abiguntur, expulse: iterum
redeunt. Tales sunt homines inquieti, qui sabbatum spiritale obseruare,
80 id est, bonis operibus studere, et orationi insistere nolunt.
Quartum preceptum, *honora patrem tuum*: et quarta plaga canina
musca (Ex 8:20–32). Caninum est enim non agnoscere parentes. Unde
qui parentes non ueneratur: / merito pena canum multatur.
Quintum *non mechaberis*. Quinta plaga *mors* (166v) *in peccora*
85 (Ex 9:1–7). Qui enim uxori aut filie aliene insidiatur: uictus
cupiditate bestiarum tamquam amisso homine erit pecus, non natura;
sed in homine habens similitudinem pecoris: dum non uult intelligere.
Nolite fieri sicut equus et mulus (Ps 31:9): quasi, si pecus
esse non times; uel mori sicut pecus time.
90   Sextum preceptum. *Non occides*. Sexta plaga *pustule in corpore*:
et uesice bullientes (Ex 9:8–12). Tales sunt anime homicidarum:
ardent ira et iracundia. O si possemus uidere animas homicidarum:
plus plangeremus quam putrescentia corpora ulceratorum!
Septimum preceptum *non furabis*: et plaga septima *grando in*
95 *fructibus* (Ex 9:13–35). Quod per furtum contra preceptum domini
subducis: de celo perdis. Nemo enim habet iniustum lucrum: sine

---

66. B. inv. ueritati christiane. 69 & 76. BV cynifes. 86–89. V peccus, peccoris. 95. B
fructum.

to worship God the Creator. By reverencing creatures in place of the Creator, they attributed to a creature what belongs to God. Those who deny christian truth, and being themselves, in their vanity deceive others, are frogs; they weary the ears, without feeding the mind.

Against violation of the sabbath 'gnats' multiplied, (Ex 8:16–19), restless insects, which never slumber. These are excessive cares and grievous anxieties, which torment those who do not know how to rest in God. The restless react against the Holy Spirit and are endlessly involved in earthly affairs. To them applies the saying: the burdens of this life made them miserable and they can not enjoy the sabbath, that is, a rest. Instead of their restlessness, the just ought to enjoy a sabbath in their hearts and the sanctifying of the Holy Spirit. But 'gnats' are the tiniest insects. Flying restlessly, irregularly, they do not allow us to relax. While we swat at them, they disappear, only to return again. Like gnats are restless persons. They are unwilling to enjoy a spiritual sabbath, that is, to attend to good works and be devoted to prayer.

Here is the fourth commandment: 'honor your father, and so forth,' and the fourth plague is a 'swarm of *wasps*, snapping like mad dogs' (Ex 8:20–32). For it is like a mad dog not to acknowledge one's parents. Hence the verses:

> If your parents you will slight,
> You shall feel the gadfly bite.

This is the fifth commandment: 'you shall not commit adultery' and the fifth plague is 'death among the beasts' (Ex 9:1–7). One who sets his cap for a neighbor's wife or daughter, overcome with bestial lust and forsaking our human estate, will be a beast not by nature but by having in person the likeness of a beast, refusing to understand the warning: 'do not be stupid like a horse or a mule' (Ps 31:9); as if he had said: if you do not fear to live as a beast, at least fear to die as a beast.

This is the sixth commandment: 'you shall not kill,' and the sixth plague: 'boils and open sores' (Ex 9:8–12). Such are the souls of homicides. They boil with anger and wrath. O! if we could only see the souls of homicides, we would lament them more than the decaying bodies of lepers.

This is the seventh commandment: 'you shall not steal,' and the seventh plague is 'hail in the crops' (Ex 9:13–35). What you filch by thieving against the Lord's commandment, you lose from heaven. No one keeps an unjust profit without a just loss. The thief may acquire a

iusto damno. Qui furatur, uerbi gratia, acquirit uestem: sed
celesti iudicio perdit fidem. Ergo qui suo malo desiderio furatur
forinsecus: iusto dei iudicio grandinatur intrinsecus.
100   Octauum preceptum, *non falsum testimonium dices*. Octaua plaga
locusta (Ex 10:1–20), animal dente nociuum. Quid autem uult falsus
testis nisi nocere mordendo; et consumere mentiendo? Et ideo nos
admonet apostolus ne nos falsis criminibus ap-(167r)-petamus. *Si*
inquit *mordetis inuicem et comeditis: uidete ne abinuicem consumamini*
105   (Gal 5:15).
　　　　Nonum preceptum: *non concupisces uxorem proximi tui*. Nona
plaga *dense tenebre* (Ex 10:21–29). Uere dense sunt tenebre. Nichil
enim sic dolet in corde patientis: quomodo si uxor eius appetatur.
Alia mala solent homines patienter accipere. Hoc autem nescio utrum
110   umquam inueniri potuerit, qui patienter ferret. O quam densas
tenebras patiuntur: qui talia perpetrant: et talia concupiscunt!
　　　　Decimum preceptum, *non concupisces rem proximi tui*. Huic con-
traria est decima plaga *mors primogenitorum*. Omnes res quas habent
homines, heredibus seruant: et in heredibus nichil primogenitis
115   carius. Qui ergo res alienas concupiscit: non uult ut habeat heredes:
in quibus nichil carius primogenitis. Qui ergo concupiscis res
alienas, et non uis illum habere heredem: ut tibi iure debeantur:
merito perdis primogenita tua, ut nec habeas heredem cui illa
dimittas. Primogenita cordis nostri: fides est. Nemo enim bonum
120   operatur: nisi fides precesserit. Qui ergo rem alienam occulte
concupiscit: internam fidem perdit.
　　　　Hec comparatio et quodammodo contrarietas decem preceptorum
et decem plagarum cautos (167v) faciat, ut habeamus securi res nostras
in preceptis dei. Horum preceptorum primum, prohibet subreptionem.
125   Secundum, errorem. Tercium, interficit seculi amorem. Quartum,
impietatem. Quintum, allidit fornicationem. Sextum, crudelitatem.
Septimum, rapacitatem. Octauum, falsitatem. Nonum, adulterii co-
gitationem. Decimum, mundi cupiditatem. Si hec diligenter atten-

---

98. V finem. 99. B dampnatur. 103. CV ammonet. 104. V inquid. 106. B om. plaga.
109. B om. patienter. 110–11. V om. tenebras. 116–17. B Qui ergo res alienas concupiscis et non uis illum heredem, V Cum ergo concupiscis res alienas et non uis ullum
habere heredem. 120. V aliam. 122. BV inv. .x. preceptorum contrarietas et .x. 126. B
allicit. 127. V Octauam perimit falsitatem. 128. V inv. mundi cupiditatem.

cloak, for example, but he loses this credit in the heavenly balance. Hence one who by his evil desire steals publicly, 'will feel the hail' inwardly through the just judgement of God.

This is the eighth commandment: 'you shall not bear false witness' and the eighth plague is 'the locust,' an insect with a ravenous tooth (Ex 10:1–20). What is the intention of a false witness, if not to harm by back-biting and to consume by lies? Therefore the apostle warns us against an appetite for false charges: 'if you bite and devour one another, take heed lest you be consumed by one another' (Gal 5:15).

This is the ninth commandment: 'you shall not covet your neighbor's spouse,' and the ninth plague is 'impenetrable darkness' (Ex 10:21–29). This darkness really is impenetrable. Nothing so rankles in the heart of the aggrieved, as another's lust for one's spouse. Persons are wont to accept other offences with patience, but I do not know, if anyone could ever be found who would patiently endure this. What dense darkness they endure, who long for and accomplish such crimes!

This is the tenth commandment: 'you shall not covet your neighbor's goods and to match it is the tenth plague, 'the death of the firstborn.' All the possessions we own, we keep for our heirs, and among our heirs none is dearer than the firstborn. Hence you who covet your neighbor's goods, do not wish him to have any heirs, among whom none is dearer than the firstborn, that in law his goods may be owed to you; rightly you forfeit your own birthright, that you may have no heir to receive it. The birthright of our heart is our faith, for no one does good works unless his faith has led the way. Hence one who inwardly covets another's goods, loses his inmost faith.

This comparison and somehow this contradistinction between the ten commandments and the ten plagues should make us cautious, that we may keep our possessions in peace, relying on the commandments of God. The first commandment forbids robbery and the second deception. The third kills love of the world and the fourth impiety. The fifth destroys fornication, the sixth cruelty, the seventh greed, the eighth falsehood, the ninth the thought of adultery and the tenth covetousness of the world. If we carefully observe these precepts, in our desire to

dimus, ut que sunt mala fugere, et que sunt bona auxiliante domino
130 uoluerimus exercere: erimus populus dei, et de iniqua egyptiorum
seruitute, id est, spiritalium nequitiarum persecutione liberati,
(Eph 6:12) ad terram promissionis poterimus feliciter perueniri.

---

130. C egiptiorum. 131. V spiritualium. 132. V om. terram, add. eternam.

avoid evil and to do good with the Lord's help, we shall be the people of God, freed from wicked enslavement to the Egyptians, that is, from the persecution of spiritual villains (Eph 6:12), and able to arrive happily at the land of promise.

❦

III. SERLO OF SAVIGNY, A PRELATE, LIKE THE
FRUIT OF AN OLIVE TREE

The texts and spirit of this short passage strongly resemble those in the first passage above on the apostles Peter and Paul.

The qualities expected of a prelate chosen by the people of God are indicated through the symbols of the text. He is not the red berry from a hawthorn bush but the green olive of the olive tree, He produces oil to light his lamp and shines on all who are in the house of God.

A prelate elected with these qualities would be a rejoinder to the badinage of any who rejoiced to recall Cis as a harsh father or the Cistercians with their resticity and austerity, the Harshtercians.

III. No. 35, added to Wilmart's List, (J), Oxford Bodleian,
Jesus College, MS 19, f. 12, c. 2.

(Rubric:) Item, De oliueto prelatus sumi debeat non spineto;
(Margin:) Item, Quod de oliueto prelatus sumi debeat non spineto.
Precipe filiis israel, ut afferant tibi oleum de arboribus
oliuarum purissimum piloque tusum, ut ardeat lucerna semper in tha-
5 *bernaculo testimonii extra uelum quod appansum* etc. (Ex 27.20–21,
Lev 24.2). *Oleum a filiis israel,* quoniam significat: uir gratia
spiritus sancti et pietate et misericordia plenus a tanto populo
eligitur. Suscipitur autem de arboribus oliuarum, id est, de doctrina
congregatus (marg.) et contemplacione sanctorum, quatenus et
10 pacem diligat et sanctorum patrum dulcedinem et saporem imitetur.
Sic autem uita et moribus purus, et sicut apostolus ait, *irreprehensibilis*
(1 T 3:4), sic quoque *pilo contusus,* non delicatus, nec
ociosus, sed in tribulacione et in iniuriis per pacienciam probatus,
(Rom 12:12) et iste quidem ad hoc eligitur, *ut ardeat lucerna*
15 *semper in thabernaculo testimonii* (Ex 28:43), ut nunquam thaberna-
culum sine lucerna, numquam cubiculum sine sit lumine, ut nunquam
prepositus sit sine exposicione et doctrina. Ipse enim lucerna.
Ipse sit oleo plenus. Ipse sit misericordia et pietate repletus.
Debet autem hec lucerna *ardere extra uelum* ut ab omnibus uideatur,
20 et omnes illuminet, et secundum euangelium *luceat omnibus qui in*
domo sunt (Mt 5:15).

---

13. *Ipsa ruina, est medicina,* similiter cadens cujusdam auctoris nescio.

IV. NO. 35, ADDED TO WILMART'S LIST, (J)

A Prelate, like the fruit of the olive tree (Rubric and margin). By the same [Serlo of Savigny]: that a prelate should be the fruit of an olive tree and not of a thorn bush.

'Command the children of Israel to bring you the purest oil from olive trees, crushed in a mortar, that their lamp may ever shine in the tabernacle of testimony, outside the veil, and so forth' (Ex 27:20–21, Lev 24:2). 'Oil from the children of Israel,' because this means that a man filled with the grace and piety and mercy of the holy Spirit, is being chosen by such a great people. But he is plucked from olive trees, that is, gathered from the teaching and contemplation of the saints, in as far as he loves peace and imitates the goodness and savor of the holy fathers. Thus innocent in life and character and as the apostle says: 'irreproachable' (1 T 3:4), thus also 'crushed in the mortar,' and not soft or idle, but with patience tested in trial and insult (Rom 12:12), he is indeed a man chosen for this purpose: 'that his lamp may ever shine in the tabernacle of testimony, that the tabernacle may never be without its lamp or the room without light, and that he may never be a leader without doctrine and example. Yes, he is the lamp. Let him be filled with oil. Let him overflow with mercy and devotion. But this lamp should shine 'outside the veil,' to be seen by all, to enlighten all, and according to the gospel, 'let the lamp enlighten all in the house' (Mt 5:15).

IV. MASTER SERLO, 'FOR THE JUST, ALL'S WELL,'

ETON COLLEGE, MS 39

The one term of address, *fratres mei*, suggests that the sermon was meant for fellow-monks. After the text, the first word, *Simplicitas*, is a favorite cistercian word: an attribute of God, and an attribute of cistercian style in life and letters, in art and architecture. In this short sermon the bible is cited at least forty-nine times but without chapter or verse: twenty-three of these are from the Old Testament. The one other author cited at lines 30–31, and 173, is Isidore of Seville. Rhetorical figures abound: anaphora and rime, doublets like parallel clauses in the psalms and numberless triads or triple clauses, symbols of the Trinity.

In the familiar cistercian metaphors of ruminant or nurse, the author chews every word. Here, 'the just,' means the righteous as opposed to the wicked, not *uir* but *homo*, which is developed in the following paragraphs: 1. Serlo masticates every word of the text. 2. The just is defined as a person of faith, who believes not in vanities but in ultimate reatlities. 3. This faith makes three demands: to believe in God's existence, his teaching and his love, *credere deum, credere deo, credere in deum*, (figure of *traductio*), 4. God's existence inspires awe, his teaching hope, while his creative love seeks a return from our hearts. 5–7. With multiple triads and passages from scripture, Serlo leads through the purgative to the illuminative and unitive ways: *timore correcti, spe sulleuati, possumus tantum proficere ut deum diligamus*. 8–10. The text is applied to the just in life, in death and after death. 11. The brethren are counselled not to be remiss in following the just who are faithful, because for the just 'all's well' *in bono quod subest, in bono quod inest, in bono quo coest, in bono quo preest*.

IV. Windsor, Eton College MS 39, ff. *46v–48r*
Sermo Magistri Serlonis de iusto homine bene uiuente
 (1) Dicite iusto quoniam bene (Is 3:10). Simplicitas dicti
sine determinatione: sine uerbi appositione multiplicem constituit
intellectum. Iusto semper bene est: fuit et erit. Iusto bene est
in celo et in terra: et apud inferos. Iusto bene est in prosperis:
5 in aduersis. Semper et ubique: iusto bene est. Item. Dixit dominus
angelis. *Dicite iusto quoniam bene est,* scilicet ei: ad iocunditatem.
Dixit hominibus, *quoniam bene,* ad correctionem. Dixit
diabolo et satellitibus eius, *dicite iusto quoniam bene:* ad confusionem.
Iusto bene est: in statu, in casu, in correctione. In
10 statu: ut qui stat, *videat ne cadat* (1 Cor 10:12). In casu: quia
si *cediderit* iustus *non collidetur* (Ps 36:24). In correctione: quia
si ceciderit iustus forcior resurgit (Pr 24:16). Ipsa Ruina: iusto
est medicina. *Omnia enim cooperantur in bonum: his qui secundum
propositum uocati sunt sancti* (Rm 8:28).
15 (2) Quis est iste iustus? Scriptum est: *quia iustus ex fide
uiuit* (Rm 1:17). Iustus iste cui bene est: fidem ex fide sua consequitur.
Est enim fides *substancia rerum sperandarum argumentum
non apparentium* (Heb 11:1). Res autem mundane sperande non sunt:
quia uane sunt. Uane quidem; quia uanescunt et transeunt: et diu
20 permanere non possunt. *Preterit enim figura huius mundi* (1 Cor 7:
31). Et ille sapientissimus regum deprehendit omnia *uanitatem essse
et afflictionem spiritus* (Eccles 2:11). Unde nec incongrue dicitur
uanum: quasi uadens ad nichilum. Rerum ergo mundanarum non est
propter leuitatem sui aliqua substantia: quia illarum non est aliqua
25 constancia (Sap 5:1). Res quidem celestes quia permanenciam
habent, et ueritatem: substantiam habent que fides est. Que ideo
sperande sunt: quia uideri non possunt: *Argumentum non apparentium*
(Heb 11:1). Probat enim fides: non apparentia esse. Unde et argumentum, quasi argute men-(c. 2)-tis inuentum dicitur. Arguta enim
30 mens et subtilis que inuenit non apparentia esse apparentia! Apparentia
uero non apparentia, sed transeuntia. Utique qui hanc fidem
habet, mundum contemnit. Qui mundum contempnit: uitam inuenit;
et ita *iustus ex fide uiuit* (Rm 1:17).

28–29. *Argumentum:* Isidori Etymologiarum VI, viii, 16.

IV MASTER SERLO, 'FOR THE JUST, ALL'S WELL'

(1) 'Tell the just that all's well' (Is 3:10). The simplicity of this command without added verse or further word, prompts many a reflection. For the just, it always is, was and will be well. For the just all's well in heaven, on earth and under the earth. For the just, all's well in prosperity or in adversity. Always and everywhere, for the just all's well. Again, the Lord said to the angels: 'say to the just that all's well,' that is, speak to the just for his comfort. He said to men: 'all's well,' for their amendment. He said to the devil and his minions: 'say to the just, all's well,' to confound them. 'All's well for the just,' when he is upright or fallen or chastened; when upright, since he who stands, 'should take heed lest he fall' (1 Co 10:12): when fallen, for though the just may fall, 'he will not be cast headlong' (Ps 36:24); and when chastened, for 'though the just may fall, he rises all the stronger' (Pr 24:16). Even ruin is good medicine for the just, 'because everything conspires for the good of those, who according to God's purpose have been called to be saints' (Rm 8:28).

(2) But who is the just? Paul says that 'the just lives by faith' (Rm 1:17). The just for whome 'all's well,' acquires faith from his own faith, 'for faith is the assurance of things hoped for, the conviction of what is not seen' (Heb 11:1). Worldly goods are not worth hoping for, because they are vain. They really are vain, because they vanish and pass away and cannot long endure, 'for the form of this world is passing away' (1 Co 7:31). The wisest of kings perceived that 'all is as vain as trying to harness the wind' (Qo 2:11). Not ineptly then, is the world called 'vain,' since it is vanishing into nothingness. Hence there is no substance to worldly goods, thanks to their instability because they are inconstant (Ws 5:1). Now goods of heaven, because they have permanence and truth, have the substance which is faith. They should be hoped for, because they cannot be seen: 'the argument of the unseen' (Heb 11:1). Faith indeed proves that things not apparent do exist. Hence also an argument is called the discovery (c. 2) of an acute mind. For the mind is acute and subtle which discovers that things not apparent are apparent. Yet these apparent things are not apparent but transient. Certainly one who has this faith, despises the world. One who despises the world finds life, and so 'the just lives by faith' (Rm 1:17).

(3) Sed hec fides: tres articulos habet. Debemus enim secundum
35 dum hanc fidem credere deum, credere deo, credere in deum. Credere
deum est credere eum esse: non sicut insipiens: qui dixit *in corde
suo non est deus* (Ps 13:1). Sed credere eum esse et tante potestatis
esse, ut uerbo omnia ex nichilo creauerit: tantum et talem ut
nemo ei resistere possit. Credere deo est uerbis et doctrine eius
40 acquiescere, credere uera esse que in uita docuit. Credere in deum
est toto mentis affectu in ipsum tendere, et uite propositum in
ipsum dirigere.

    (4) Primus articulus: timorem incutit. Secundus: spem. Tercius
dilectionem. Eum enim non uereri qui summa maiestas summa po-
45 tentia est, qui potest corpus et animam mittere in gehennam ignis
(Mt 10:28); eum inquam non uereri: summa dementia est. Eius doctrine et uerbis non acquiescere qui summa sapientia est que *ex ore
altissimi* (Eccli 24:5) processit, *qui fundauit terram scientia*, et
stabiliuit celos prudentia (Pr 3:19) eius uerbis et promissionibus
50 non confidere: summa est miseria. Eum non diligere, qui *prior dilexit
nos* (1 Jo 4:19), qui proprio *filio suo non perpercit, sed pro
nobis omnibus tradidit illum* (Rm 8:32); qui eciam omnia cum filio
largitatus est, eum toto cordis affectu non diligere: maxima certe
ingratitudo est. Timeamus ergo ipsum, speremus in ipsum, diligamus
55 ipsum, per quem omnia, in quo omnia, sine quo nulla (Rm 11:36).

    (5) Hunc triplicem affectum trinus et unus deus in ueteri
testamento tribus in locis tripliciter nobis insinuauit: per triplicem
sacrificiorum locum, tres (f. 47r, c. 1) modos spiritualiter
sacrificandi ostendens. Sacrificabatur enim in atrio ante templum:
60 in templo eciam ante uelum; in sanctis sanctorum intra uelum. Hec
erant tria loca sacrificiorum: et in singulis trium tria continebantur.
In atrio erat altare eneum (Exod 38:30); uter plenus aqua
(Exod 40:28): gradus quindecim (Exod 20:26). In altari cremabantur
carnes hostiarum; et significat formidinem pene: ex cuius recordatione
65 caro conteritur. Unde illud. *Confige timore tuo carnes meas*

Linea 53. ms, *maxime*. Linea 75. ms, *fortitudinem*, ex linea 64 vero rectius legitur *formidinem pene*.

(3) This faith has three parts, because according to this faith we ought to believe in God, to believe God and to trust God. To believe in God is first of all to believe that God exists, unlike the fool who said in his heart 'there is no God' (Ps 13:1). It is to believe that God exists, that he is of such power, that with one word he created everything from nothing, and that he is of such greatness and quality, that no one can resist him. To believe in God is secondly to believe his words and his teaching, to believe the truth of what he taught in his lifetime. To trust god is thirdly to hasten towards him with the full affection of one's mind and to direct towards him the whole purpose of one's life.

(4) Of the three parts, God's existence inspires awe, his teaching hope, his love affection. Not to be in awe of him, who is the supreme Majesty, the supreme Power, 'who can send both body and soul to the gehenna' of fire (Mt 10:28), not to fear him, I repeat, is supreme folly. Not to assent to his teaching and his words, who is the supreme Wisdom, which proceeds 'from the mouth of the most high' (Si 24:5), who 'by knowledge founded the earth and by understanding established the heavens (Pr 3:19), not to trust his words and promises is supreme misery. Not to love him 'who first loved us' (1 Jn 4:19), who 'did not spare his own Son but gave him up for us all' (Rm 8:32), and who shared everything with his Son, not to love him with the heart's full affection, certainly is the height of ingratitude. Let us fear him then, hope in him, and love him, through whom all things exist, in whom all exist, without whom nothing exists (Rm 11:36).

(5) The triune god has suggested for us this threefold affection in a triple way in three places in the Old Testament. For through the three sites for sacrifice (f. 47r, c. 1) he shows three sites for making spiritual sacrifices. Sacrifice was offered: in the atrium before the temple, also in the temple in front of the veil and behind the veil in the Holy of Holies. These were the three sites for sacrifice and in each of the three sites were three fixtures. In the atrium were: a bronze altar (Ex 38:30), an urn full of water (Ex 40:28) and fifteen steps (Ex 20:26). On the altar was burned the flesh of the victims to symbolize the dread of punishment, for in recalling the penalty, the flesh is crushed as the psalmist says: 'crush my

domine (Ps 118:120). In utre aqua pleno lauabantur sacerdotes in-
gressuri templum (Exod 40:29): et significat confessionem culpe:
que accenditur ex lacrimarum inundatione. Per gradus in templum
ascendebant: et ascensio graduum correctionem uite significat. Et
70 bene quindecim erant. Quindenarius enim: in septem et octo diuiditur.
Per castitatem et iusticiam: corrigenda est uita peccatoris.
Septenarius enim numerus est uirginalis; octonarius: numerus iusticie.
Sed uterque quietem significat. Septenarius quietem que est
in spe: octonarius, quietem que est in re. Timor ergo hec tria
75 operatur: formidinem pene; confessionem culpe; correctionem uite:
et hec ex fide qua credimus deum esse.
  (6) Timor eciam iste qui ita excruciat: sacrificium est in
atrio: non in templo. Unde. *Perfecta caritas: foras mittit timorem*
(1 Jn 2:18). Sed post hunc timorem, bene introitur in templum:
80 in quo secundus erat locus sacrificiorum: in quo erant, mensa
cum panibus (Exod 40:20); candelabrum cum lucernis (40:22); et
altare aureum, cum thimiamate (40:24). Mensa qua reficiebantur
sacerdotes, uitam christi significat: qui exemplo suo nos reficit.
Exemplum enim dedit nobis: ut et nos ita faciamus (Jn 13:15).
85 Candelabrum autem (significat) doctrinam eius: qui septiformi
gracia spiritus sancti reficiens, *illuminat omnem hominen uenientem
in hunc mundum* (Jn 1:9). In mundum: scilicet iusticie. *In mundo
erat*: mundo scilicet innocen-(c. 2)-tie; *et mundus eum non cognouit*
(Jn 1:10): mundus malicie. Altare aureum in quo thimiama
90 accendebatur: mortem christi similiter significat; qua seipsum
christus obtulit deo patri pro salute nostram hostiam uiuam et ueram:
in odorem suauitatis (Exod 29:41). Christus ergo mensa fuit
proposicionis uiuendo (Exod 25:23–30): candelabrum docendo (Exod
25: 31–40): altare thimiamatis moriendo (1 Par 6:49). Spem ergo
95 ponamus in uita eius; in doctrina; in morte; et hoc deo credendo:
timore ita correcti, spe sulleuati, ad sancta sanctorum ascendere
possumus, in tantum scilicet proficere, ut deum diligamus et merito
quoniam ibi tria sunt, propiciatorium, archa testamenti, cherubim

---

73–74. *Septenarius, quietem que est in spe:*
      octonarius, quietem que est in re. similiter cadens, cujusdam auctoris nescio; cf.
etiam lineam 163: quia gratulantur, quod in re possessuri sunt, quod in spe
desiderauerant.

flesh with your fear, O Lord (Ps 118:120).' In the urn full of water, the priests about to enter the temple were wont to wash (Ex 40:29); this symbolizes the confession of one's fault, which follows on the flood of tears. Priests used to ascend into the temple by the steps and this ascent of the steps signifies the amendment of one's life. Happily there were fifteen steps, for fifteen is the sum of seven and eight. Through chastity and justice the life of the sinner is to be amended, for seven is a number for virginity and eight a number of justice. But both signify repose: seven the repose which exists in hope, eight the repose which exists in realization. Fear then produces these three: the dread of punishment, the confession of guilt, and amendment of life, and these three are consequences of the faith by which we believe in the existence of God.

(6) The fear so excruciating, is also the sacrifice in the atrium but not in the temple, where 'perfect love casts out fear' (1 Jn 2:18). After this fear one makes a good entrance into the temple, in which is the second site for sacrifices; there were the table with loaves, the candlestick with lamps and the golden altar with incense (Ex 40:20–24). The table at which the priests were nourished signifies the life of Christ, who by his example nourishes us, for he gave us an example that we should imitate (Jo 13:15). The candlestick signifies the teaching of the one who by nourishing us with the sevenfold grace of the holy Spirit, 'illumines every one who comes into this world' (Jn 1:9), the world of innocense (c. 2), 'yet the world know him not' (Jn 1:10), the world of wickedness. The golden altar on which the incense was enkindled, signifies likewise the death of Christ, whereby for our salvation he offered himself to God the Father, our living and true victim, as an appeasing fragrance (Ex 29:41). By living, then, Christ was the table of propitiation (Ex 25:23–30); by teaching, the candlestick (Ex 25:31–40); by dying, the altar of incense (1 Par 6:49). Let us place our hope then, in his life, his teaching, his death, and this by believing in God. Thus corrected by fear and elevated by hope, we can ascend to the Holy of Holies, that is, we can make such progress as to love God, and rightly, since the three fixtures are there: the propitiatory, the ark of the testament and the cherubim with wings

alis expansis ad uolandum (3 R 6:27).

100   (7) Propiciatorium significat perfectam remissionem peccatorrum:
ex qua deus diligendus est. Tanto enim amplius diligere eum
debemus: quanto ipse nobis plura remiserit. Sed et ipsa dilectio
dilectis causa remissionis est. Caritas enim excoquit rubiginem
peccatorum. Unde. Demissa sunt *ei peccata multa: quoniam dilexit*
105   *multum* (Lc 7:47). Archa uero in qua continebatur lex domini, cogni-
cionem dei significat: ad quam post emundacionem peccatorum accedi-
tur. Soli enim illi deum uidere possunt: quibus mundatus est interior
oculus mentis. Unde. *Beati mundo corde: quoniam ipsi deum*
videbunt (Mt 5:8). Hec autem dei cognicio: causa est dilectionis.
110   Quis enim emundatorem suum saluatorem bonorum omnium collatorem
iam cognitum non diligat? Numquid medicum suum non diliget cecus, si
utriusque oculi uisum, uel saltem alterius gratis sibi restituat?
Quanto brucior est omni animali qui deum non diligit: qui sibi gehennam
remisit; anime cecitatem abstersit; uiam qua ad celum evolet
115   ostendit! Unde et cherub alis expansis ad uolandum: significat quoniam
post ista nichil aliud restat nisi ut (f. 47v, c. 1) ad celum
toto mentis anhelitu euolemus; toto desiderio tendamus; non leui
non remisso sed cum paulo dicamus. Cupio *dissolui: et esse cum*
christo (Phil 1:23). Propheta eciam simili desiderio accensus:
120   clamans et eiulans dicit. *Heu michi quia incolatus meus prolongatus*
est (Ps 119:5). Et hec consequimur ex fide: qua in deum credimus.
Cum ergo iustus timore compunctus, spe erectus, dilectione
deo coniunctus fuerit: dicite ei *quoniam bene.*

(8) Bene est ei eciam in uita; bene in morte: bene post mortem.
125   Bene in uita; quia si contigerint aduersa: non deprimitur.
Si prospera: non extollitur. Si persecutionem patitur propter iusticiam:
scit quod premium erit regnum celorum (Mt 5:10). Rerum
suarum ablatione, carnis eciam maceratione, non mouetur. Consolatur
enim ipsum paulus dicens. Quoniam *non sunt condigne passiones*
130   *huius temporis ad futuram gloriam que reuelabitur in nobis* (Rm 8:
18). Quinimo de his magis confidit. Quanto enim uia durior fuerit:
tanto securius incedit. Lutosa uia, quanto mollior: tanto periculosior.
Unde propheta. *Propter uerba labiorum tuorum ego custodiui*

Lineis 102–3. ms, *dilectis*; attamen super litteras 'is' scribitur littera 'o'; unde sensus esse
videtur: ipsa dilectio dilectis causa remissionis est.

outstretched to fly (3 K 6:27).

(7) The propitiatory means the perfect remission of sins, whereupon God is to be loved. Indeed we ought to love him more, the more numerous the sins he has forgiven us. Even love itself is a reason for the remission of sin for the beloved, for perfect love burns off the rust of sin, wherefore 'many sins were forgiven her, because she loved much' (Lk 7:47). But the ark of the testament, wherein was contained the Law of the Lord, means the knowledge of God, which one approaches after the purification of sins. Only they can see God, whose mind's inner eye has been purified. Therefore, 'blessed are the pure of heart, for they will see God' (Mt 5:8). The knowledge of God is a reason for love, for once he is known, who would not love this purifier, his savior and the donor of all blessings? Will the blind man not love his doctor, who gratuitously restores to him the sight of both eyes or of one at least? How much more brutish than any brute is one who does not love the God who forgave him the punishment of gehenna and who wiped away the blindness of his soul, to show him the way to soar to heaven! Hence the cherub with wings extended for flight means that at journey's end nothing remains but (f. 47v, c. 1) to soar to heaven with every yearning of our minds, and to progress with no slight nor slack velleity but with full longing, and to say with Paul: I desire 'to be dissolved and to be with Christ' (Phil 1:23). Enkindled with a similar desire, the prophet also cried aloud and lamented: 'woe is me, that my sojourn is prolonged' (Ps 119:5). These blessings we derive from the faith, through which we believe in God's love. Therefore, when the just has been touched by fear, encouraged by hope and joined to God by love, tell him that all's well.

(8) For the just all's well also in life, in death and after death. All's well in life, for if one meets adversity, one is not downcast; if one meets prosperity, one is not puffed up. If one suffers persecution for justice's sake, one knows his reward will be the kingdom of heaven (Mt 5:10). He is not moved by the loss of his possessions nor even by the torture of his flesh, for Paul consoles him with the words: 'the sufferings of this time are not worth comparing with the glory to be revealed in us' (Rm 8:18). Rather, thanks to these he shows greater confidence, for the harder the road the more carefree he is on his journey; the softer and more slippery the road, the more perilous the journey. Hence the prophet says: 'thanks to the words on your lips, I kept an eye on the ways of

uias duras (Ps 16:4). Unde et sponsus in canticis hinnulo cervorum
135 comparatur. Qui *uenit saliens in montibus transiliens colles* (Cant
2.8). Hac eciam una sola christus queritur: hac sola invenitur.
Christus enim non nisi in cruce inueniri potest. Unde, *qui uult*
uenire post me, abneget semetipsum: et tollat crucem suam, et sequatur
me (Mt 16:24). De his omnibus: gloriatur iustus. Unde *si*
140 *gloriari oportet: que infirmitatis mee sunt gloriabor* (2 Cor 11:
30). Cum de his omnibus confidat, magis, magisque glorietur: *Dicite*
iusto, quoniam bene.
      (9) Iusto enim uita is- (c. 2) -ta carcer est: mors huius
carceris solutio. Nemo enim hic adeo iustus est: ut perfectam
145 possit hic consequi iusticiam. Unde paulus, quia bonum quod uoluit
perfecte implere non potuit: exclamat. *Infelix ego homo; quis me*
liberabit de corpore mortis huius? (Rm 7:24) Expeditus ergo mole
carnis euolet ad deum: et a curru certaminis currum ascendit glori-
ficationis. Sicut et de rege Iuda legitur, quia cum in curru suo
150 pugnaret pro lege domini uulneratus est ad mortem; et a curru illo
translatus est in alium, a quo transductus est in Ierusalem: (2 Par 35:24) ita
unusquisque iustus in corpore suo dimicans contra potestates tenebrarum
harum; contra spirituales nequitias in celestibus (Eph 6:
12). *Est enim milicia uita hominis super terram* (Jb 7:1). Deinde
155 uulnere mortis percutitur; et carne deposita ascendit uehiculum
angelorum: et per manus ipsorum deportatur in uisionem pacis.
      (10) Unde. *In leticia egredimini: in pace deducemini. Montes*
et colles: cantabunt coram uobis laudes . . . Pro saliunca, ascendet
abies; pro uirga heremi, cedrus libani: *et pro urtica crescet*
160 *mirtus* (Is 55:12–13). Sed quid faciet uirgula heremi; ubi tremore
concutietur cedrus libani (Eccli 16:19)? *In leticia egrediuntur*
sancti de corpore, quasi in dilatatione cordis (Pr 21:4): quia
gratulantur quod in re possessuri sunt, quod in spe prius disidera-
uerant. *In pace deducuntur*: quia post mortem istam non affliguntur.
165 *Montes et colles cantabunt coram uobis laudem*: quia maiores et minores
angeli ymnum triumphi et uictorie eis cantabunt. *Pro saliunca*
ascendet abies: et cetera. Saliunca herba humilis est: que humilitatem

---

149. *De rege iuda*: i.e. Josias, 2 Par 35:24. 174. Isid. *idem* XVII, vii, 32.

the violent' (Ps 16:4). Hence the Beloved in the Song of Songs is also compared to the fawn of stags, because 'he comes loping on the mountains, bounding over the hills' (Sg 2:8). Moreover, by his one lone bride Christ is sought and by her alone he is found, for Christ can be found only on the cross. Hence, 'let him who wishes to come after me, deny himself, take up his cross and follow me' (Mt 16:24). Of all these blessings the just one boasts: yes, 'if one must boast, I will boast of what belongs to my weakness' (2 Co 11:30). Since the just may be condident about all these gifts, he may be more and more boastful: 'tell the just that all's well.'

(9) For to the just, life itself (c. 2) is a prison but death a release from prison. Indeed no one on earth is so just, that he can reach perfect justice here. Hence, because Paul could not perfectly accomplish the good he desired, he cried out; 'unhappy am I! who will free me from this body of death?' (Rm 7:24). Once released from the encumbrance of flesh, he may fly off to God and from the chariot of the arena ascend the chariot of glory. Just as we read about (Josias), the king of Judah: when he was fighting in his chariot for the law of the Lord, he was mortally wounded and transferred from his own to another chariot, in which he was carried to Jerusalem (2 Par 35:24), so each and every just one in his body contends against the powers of the present darkness, against the wickedness of the spirits in the heavens (Eph 6:12). 'Mortal life upon earth is really warfare' (Jb 7:1). When one is mortally wounded and, abandoning his flesh, ascends the angel's carriage, one is carried by their hands into the vision of peace.

(10) Hence 'you go out in joy and will be led forth in peace. Mountains and hills will sing praises in your presence . . . In place of the briar, the silver fir will spring up;' in place of Herem's rod, the cedar of Lebanon; 'and in place of the nettle the myrtle will flourish' (Is 55:12–13). But what will become of the rod of Herem, when the cedar of Lebanon will be struck and tremble? (Si 16:19). From their bodies the saints arise in joyfullness, as if their hearts were bursting with gratitude (Pr 21:4), since they boast that they are about to posess in reality what previously they had desired in hope. 'They are led forth in peace, because after their death they are not afflicted. 'Mountains and hills will sing praise in your presence,' because the angels, both the greater and the less, will sing for them a hymn of triumph and victory. 'In place of the briar, the silver fir will spring up,' and so forth. The briar is a lowly shrub,

sanctorum significat. (f. 48r, c. 1). Cedrus et abies arbores
sunt excelse: et in altum erecte. Unde et abies ab abeundo dicitur:
170 et significat hanc quidem sanctorum eleuationem. *Pro saliunca ergo*
ascendet abies, id est, pro humilitate quam in terris habuit erigetur
et eleuabitur usque ad solium dei. *Et pro urtica crescet mirtus*.
Urtica quedam herba est que et pungit et urit: et significat
carnem nostram. Caro enim urit nos quandoque necessitatibus famis
175 et sitis: pungit quandoque stimulis inhonestis. Sed cum *mortale hoc*
induerit immortalitatem, et corruptibile hoc incorruptionem (1 Cor
15:53–54): donabimur utraque stola; gloria scilicet carnis et anime:
et pro urtica carnis nostre, crescet nobis mirtus temperantie;
ut iam non fiat rebellio carnis aduersus spiritum: nec spiritus adversus
180 carnem.
      (11) Et uos fratres mei laborate ad iusticiam: ut et uobis
cum iusto sit in mortem bene. Nec remisse quidem uel dilatorie hoc
agendum est. Nichil enim morte cercius: nichil hora mortis incercius.
Bene est et iusto post mortem; bene est et iusto quadrupliciter.
185 Bene est ei in bono quod subest: bene est ei in bono quod
inest; bene est ei in bono quo coest: bene est ei bono quod preest.
Bono quod subest bene est ei. Gratulabitur enim se iehennam evasisse;
in quo uidet demonem et complices eius sine intermissione
torqueri: qui eum quondam in uita infestauerant. Et comparans
190 gloriam suam miserie illorum, gaudet se in illam non incidisse; et
de bono suo gracias agens saluatori: iusticiam eius in eos qui
meruerunt commendat. Unde, *letabitur iustus cum uiderit uindictam*
(Ps 57:11). Bene est ei in bono quod inest; habebit enim iustus in
summa illa beatitudine omnem uirtutem: omnem decorem; omnem afflu-
195 entiam. Erit (c.2) enim deus tunc *omnia in omnibus* (1 Cor 15:28).
Bene est ei bono quod coest; quia non ex se solo gloriabitur iustus:
sed ex societate angelorum, apostolorum et martirum magna ex-
ultatione gaudebit. Multum enim decent ei ad beatitudinem: si de
cohabitantium felicitate inuideret: uel de miseria confunderetur.
200 Bene est ei bono quod preest; dum deum facie ad faciem contempla-

---

178. Isid. *idem*. XVII, ix, 44.

which signifies the humility of the saints (f. 48, c. 1). The cedar and the silver fir are lofty trees, which raise their heads high. Moreover, the silver fir is named from soaring aloft, and really means this exaltation of the saints. 'In place of the briar, then, the silver fir will ascend;' that is, in exchange for the humility it showed on earth, it will be raised and exalted even to the throne of God. 'In place of the nettle the myrtle will grow.' The nettle is a species of plant, which both pricks and burns; it is a symbol of our flesh, for the flesh burns us at times with the pangs of hunger and thirst and goads us at times with wicked suggestions. But when 'this mortal body dons immortality and this perishable body dons imperishability (1 Co 15:53–4), we shall be adorned with both stoles, with the glory of both body and soul. To replace the nettles of our body, the myrtle of temperance will flourish in us, that there may no longer be rebellion of the flesh against the spirit or of the spirit against the flesh.

(11) Labor now for justice, my brothers, that for you also with the just all may be well in death. In this labor there should be nothing lazy or listless, for nothing is more certain than death and nothing more uncertain than the hour of death's coming. After death 'all's well for the just.' Indeed 'all's well for the just' in four ways: well for him in the good which is supposed, well for him in the good which is inherent, well for him in the good with whom he dwells, well for him in the good which prevails. All's well for him in the good which is supposed, since he is grateful for avoiding gehenna, in which he sees the demon and his minions tortured without interruption, for they once had molested him in life. Comparing his glory with their misery he rejoices that he did not fall into their misery. For his own good fortune he thanks the Savior. He commends the Savior's justice towards those who have deserved it. Therefore 'the just will rejoice, when he sees sin punished' (Ps 57:11). 'All's well for the just,' in the good which is inherent, for in that supreme happiness, the just will have all virtue, all beauty and a horn of plenty, for God will then be 'all in all' (1 Co 15:28). All's well for him in the good with whom he dwells, for the just will not boast in himself alone, but he will rejoice with great exultation in the companionship of angels and apsotles and martyrs. Indeed it greatly enhances his happiness, if he is envied for the bliss of his companions, or it casts a cloud over him, if he is taunted for their misfortune. All's well for him in the good which reigns, while he

tur; dum fontem omnium bonorum videt: a quo omnis gloria in ipsum transfunditur. Dum et in hoc maxime gratulatur: quod de societate sua deus gloriatur. Et cum in omnibus iusto sit bene: in hoc maxime. Dicite iusto Quoniam Bene.

contemplates God face to face and beholds the fountain of all blessings, from whom all glory is poured upon himself, and all the while he boasts especially in this, that God exults in his company. Now since all should be well with the just in everything, in this companionship especially tell the just that all's well.

❧❧

---

v.   FOR OR AGAINST THE LORD

B. M. SLOANE, MS 2478

In a sermon for the third Sunday of Lent Serlo comments on Lk 11:23, 'One who is not with me is against me:' as the virtues and the commandments unite us with God, so the vices and the breaking of commandments alienate us from the Lord.

Virtues: 1) One with or without the theological virtues is with or without the Lord. 2) As one who despairs minimizes the Lord's mercy, so the presumptuous minimizes his justice. 3–4) Angels and saints are one spirit with the Lord through charity, while the Son and holy Spirit enjoy the unity of essence; one who cherishes anger, hatred or envy and does not forgive, is against the Lord. 5) 'God resists the proud and gives grace to the humble.' 6) Those who persevere mightily in good, grow stronger, those who are mighty in evil will be mightily tested.

As virtues attach to and vices detach from the Lord, so do observance or breaking of the Commandments, as Serlo explains in the commandments:

    I. No one can serve God and Mammon: an idol, gluttony or greed;

    II. Taking God's name in vain or false oaths of any kind alienate us;

    III. Live sabbatically, just as the Lord rested three times;

    IV. Honor father, mother and spiritual parents: Christ and his Church;

    V. Do not kill: by deed, or thought, or by starving those in need;

    VI. Avoid all sexual activity outside the covenant of marriage;

    VII. Do not steal or filch against his will what belongs to another;

   VIII. Do not speak a false oath against your neighbor;

    IX. Do not covet in your heart your neighbor's goods;

    X. Do not covet your neighbor's wife or maidservant.

Serlo uses passages from Augustine and Isidore of Seville as a summary.

V. LONDON, B.M. SLOANE MS 2478, 73*r*–75*v*

Qui non est mecum, contra me est lucas .xi. (11.23)

(1) Sermo Magistri Serlonis dominica tercia in .xl. Qui in caritate
sunt: cum domino sunt (1 Jo 4:16). Qui uero extra caritatem: contra dominum. Et ut a primo sumamus exordium: qui credide-
5   rit, scilicet, fide formata et baptizatus fuerit, et non postea
mortaliter peccauerit: saluus erit. Et iste talis cum domino est.
Qui uero peccauerit per infidelitatem: contra dominum est, ut omnes
heretici, sicut dicitur in Io .3. (3:18). *Qui non credit: iam
iudicatus est.* Et ad ro .2. (2:12) *Qui sine lege peccauerunt:*
10   *sine lege peribunt.* Qui etiam habet firmam spem, qui incedit *ad
interiora uelaminis* sicut dicitur ad heb .6. (6:20), etiam cum domino
talis est. Qui uero peccauerit per desperacionem sicut Chaym,
sicut habetur in Gen .4. (4:13) cum dixit *maior est iniquitas mea,
quam ut ueniam merear,* uel presumpserit sicut Pharao in exo .5.
15   (5:2) cum dixit: *quis est dominus ut audiam uocem eius et dimittam
israel? nescio dominum et israel non dimittam,* non est cum domino: sed
contra dominum.

(2) Nemo utique horum eternaliter peribit. Qui autem peccauerit
in spiritum sanctum: non remittetur ei neque hic, neque in futuro,
20   sicut dicitur Mt .12. (12:32). *Sed nullus sperauit in domino
et confusus est,* ut dicitur in ecclesiastici .ii. (2:11), immo *beatus
qui confidit in domino, et erit dominus fiducia illius* ut dicitur
in ieremia .17. (17:7). Desperans enim dei misericordiam attenuat,
que tanta est: quantus est ipse deus. Secundum illud ecclesiastici
25   .2. (2:23) *secundum magnitudinem eius: sic et misericordia
eius cum ipso.* Qui uero presumit: dei attenuat iusticiam, que non
aliud quam deus iustus. Unde dicitur cor .x. Iustus est dominus *se
ipsum negare non potest* (2 Tm 2:13, 4:8), et ita non potest iusticiam
negare, qui reddet *unicuique secundum opera sua,* ut habetur
30   in apocalipsi .2. (2:23, 22:12).

(3) Similiter *qui in caritate est: cum domino est* (1 Jo
4:16). *Qui enim adheret domino: unus spiritus est,* sicut dicitur,
1 Cor .6. (6:17), scilicet, per dilectionem, sicut angeli boni et
sancti homines, non sicut filius et spiritus sanctus per essencie

v 'ONE WHO IS NOT WITH ME, IS AGAINST ME,' (LK 11:23)

A sermon of Master Serlo for the third Sunday in Lent.

(1) One who remains in charity, remains with the Lord, (1 Jn 4:16). But one who is without charity, is opposed to the Lord. Now to begin at the beginning, one who has believed with a well formed faith and has been baptised, will be saved. Such a one remains with God. But one who has sinned through lack of faith, is opposed to the Lord, as all heretics, according to John 3 (3:18), 'one who does not believe, is already condemned,' and in Romans 2 (2:12), 'those who have sinned without the law, will perish without the law.' One who has steadfast hope also remains with the Lord, for he enters 'the inner shrine behind the veil,' according to Hebrews 6 (6:20). But one who has sinned through despair like Cain, as we read in Genesis 4 (4:13), when Cain said 'my iniquity is too great for me to deserve pardon,' or one has presumed like Pharaoh in Exodus 5 (5:2), when he said: 'who is the Lord that I should heed his voice and let Israel go? I do not know the Lord and I will not let Israel go,' he is not with the Lord but against the Lord.

(2) Surely no one of these will perish forever. But one who has sinned against the holy spirit, will have his sin pardoned neither here nor in the future, as we read in Matthew 12 (12:32). But 'no one has hoped in the Lord and been confounded,' as we read in Sirach 2 (2:11). Rather 'blessed is one who trusts in the Lord, and the Lord will be his trust,' as we read in Jeremiah 17 (17:7). Indeed by despair one minimizes the mercy of God, which is as great as God himself. In the words of Sirach 2 (2:23), 'a match for God's greatness is the measure of his mercy.' But the presumptuous detract from the justice of God, which is none other than the just God. Hence we read in Corinthians 10 (*sic*, for 2 Tim 2:13), the Lord is just, 'he cannot deny himself.' 'Hence he will render to each according to his works,' as we read in Revelations 2 (2:23, 22:12).

(3) Likewise, 'one who remains in charity, remains with the Lord' (1 Jn 4:16). 'Indeed one who clings to the Lord, is one spirit with him,' as we read in 1 Corinthians 6 (6:17), namely, united through love as are good angels and saintly persons, but not united through unity of essence as the

35　unitatem. Qui uero non habent caritatem ueram, ut qui uel iram uel
　　odium uel inuidiam nutriunt: hii contra dominum sunt. *Qui enim*
　　irascitur fratri suo: dignus est gehenna. *Qui etiam dixerit*
　　fratri suo racha: erit reus concilio, scilicet congregando ut
　　iudicetur. *Qui autem dixerit fatue:* in certam, scilicet, contumeliam
40　erumpens: *reus erit gehenne ignis,* ut habetur in mattheo .5.
　　(5:22). Unde dicitur in ecclesiastico .28. (28:3), *homo homini*
　　seruat iram et a deo querit medelam quasi pro nichilo hanc a deo
　　querit qui non miseretur. Misericordia enim promissa est tantum
　　misericordibus in Mattheo .5. (5:7). *Beati misericordes quoniam*
45　*ipsi misericordiam consequuntur* et in .6. eiusdem, (6:12) *dimitte*
　　nobis debita nostra, sicut et nos dimittimus debitoribus nostris.
　　Et in Luca .6. (6:37) *dimitte et dimittetur uobis,* sicut dicitur
　　in ysaia .40. (40:2).
　　　　(4) Similiter qui odium nutriunt, contra dominum sunt. *Qui*
50　enim odit fratrem suum: homicida est, et scitis quoniam *omnis homi-*
　　cida non habet uitam eternam in se manentem, ut dicitur .1. Jo .3.
　　(3:15). Inuidi quoque non cum deo sed contra deum sunt, qui aliis
　　inuident de eorum malis gaudendo, siue de bonis eciam eorum dolen-
　　do. Hii sunt paruuli quos occidit inuidia, Job .5. (5:2).
55　　　(5) Qui etiam humiles (f. 73v) sunt: cum domino sunt. Superbi
　　uero contra dominum sunt. *Deus enim superbis resistit, humilibus*
　　autem dat graciam, sicut dicitur in .1. petri .5. (5:5). Et sunt
　　hec: superbia, ira, inuidia, spiritualia peccata: in quibus maior
　　est quam in corporalibus culpa licet minor sit infamia. *Inicium*
60　*ergo omnis peccati: superbia* sicut dicitur in ecclesiastico .x.
　　(10:15). Dicamus preter ista spiritualiter prudens, qui, scilicet,
　　scit bene conuersari et bene conuersatur *in medio praue et peruerse*
　　nacionis, ad phi .2. (2:15) cum domino est. Qui uero mouentur *omni*
　　uento doctrine, ad ephe .4. (4:14), et nunc bonorum nunc malorum
65　uestigia imitantur: contra dominum sunt. Unde dicitur in .1. Io .4.
　　(4:1) *Nolite credere omni spiritui, sed probate spiritus utrum ex*
　　deo sunt.
　　　　(6) Similiter qui fortes sunt et perseuerantes in spiritualibus:
　　cum domino sunt. *Qui enim sperant in domino: mutabunt forti-*
70　*tudinem,* sicut dicitur in ysaia .40. (40:31), scilicet, ut qui prius in
　　malo fortes fuerunt: in domino bene fortes efficiantur. E contra

Son and the holy Spirit. But they who do not have true charity, for example, those who cherish anger or hatred or envy are opposed to the Lord. 'One who is angry with his brother,' is deserving of gehenna. 'Whoever calls his brother a knave, will be brought to trial,' that is to an assembly for sentencing. 'But whoever calls his brother a fool,' that is, whoever bursts out in unabashed contumely, 'will be liable to the fire of gehenna,' as we read in Matthew 5 (5:22). Hence we read in Sirach 28, 'one harbors anger against another and yet seeks healing from the Lord!' (28:3). In vain does any one seek healing from God, while he shows no mercy, for mercy is granted only to the merciful. According to Matthew 5 (5:7), 'blessed are the merciful, for they are shown mercy.' In Matthew 6 (6:12) 'forgive us our debts, as we forgive our debtors.' In Luke 6 (6:37) 'forgive and you will be forgiven,' as we read in Isaiah 40 (40:2).

(4) Likewise, those who foster hatred, are against the Lord, 'for whoever hates his brother, is a murderer, and you know that a murderer does not have eternal life abiding in him,' as we read in 1 John 3 (3:15). The envious also are not with God but against God, for they envy others by rejoicing over their misfortunes or by grieving over their good fortunes. These are the children whom envy slays, Job 5 (5:2).

(5) Those also who are humble (f. 73v) are with the Lord, but the proud are against the Lord. 'God resists the proud, but favors the humble,' according to 1 Peter 5 (5:5). Pride, anger and envy are sins of the spirit, in which there is greater guilt though less disgrace than in sins of the body. 'The beginning of all sin is pride,' according to Sirach 10 (10:15). Let us add that one who is prudent in spirit, namely one who knows how to conduct himself well and actually does conduct himself well 'in the midst of a corrupt and perverse people,' according to Philippians 2 (2:15), is with the Lord. But those swayed 'by every wind of doctrine' Ephesians 4 (4:14), who follow the footsteps now of the good and now of the evil, are opposed to the Lord. Hence we read in 1 John 4 (4:1), 'do not believe every spirit, but test the spirits to see if they are from God.'

(6) Likewise those who are steadfast and persevere in spiritual truths are with the Lord. 'Those who hope in the Lord will advance from strength to strength, as we read in Isaiah 40 (40:31), in order that those who previously were mighty in evil, may become mighty in the Lord. But on

uero fortes in malo forcius cruciabuntur. Unde dicitur in
sapientia .6. (6:9) *fortibus forcior instat cruciatio.* Iusti
quoque per iusticiam *que perpetua est et immortalis* (Sap 1:15), ut

75 habetur in sapientia .5. (5:16) *cum domino sunt, et in perpetuum
uiuent,* quia *iustorum anime in manu dei sunt, et non tanget illos
tormentum* malicie, sicut dicitur in sapientia .3. (3:1). *Iniusti*
autem qui *disperibunt* contra dominum sunt. Et ideo simul reliquie
eorum interibunt, sicut dicitur in psalmo (36:38). Temperate eciam

80 uiuentes *qui carnem suam crucifigunt cum uiciis et concupiscenciis,*
sicut habetur ad Gal .5. (5:24). *Qui carnis curam* non faciunt *in
desideriis* ad Ro .13. (13:14) qui *spiritu facta carnis mortificauerunt*:
cum domino sunt, et ideo uiuent eternaliter, ad Romanos .8.
(8:13). E contra. Qui secundum carnem uiuunt: morientur scilicet

85 eternaliter, sicut dicitur in eodem (Rom 8:13). Sic enim uiuere
prohibet ecclesiasticus .18. (18:30) dicens: *Non eas post concupiscentias
tuas,* et in eodem (18:31). Si dederis *anime tue concupiscencias
suas:* dabit te *in gaudium inimicis tuis.*

I. Sicut itaque breuiter nunc tetigimus de uirtutibus: sic

90 eciam tangi necessarium est, et de domini preceptis sine quibus non
est salus. Unde dicitur in Mt .19. (19:16) *Si uis ingredi ad uitam:
serua mandata,* scilicet, decalogi. Qui ergo solum deum unum et
trinum adorat: pre omnibus aliis diligit et ueneratur, non faciens
sibi sculptile, non conflatile, non uentrem sibi deum faciens, sicut

95 dicitur esse, *quorum uenter est deus,* ut dicitur ad phi .3.
(3:19). *Quorum deus uenter est,* non temporalia per auariciam,
auarus enim est ydolorum seruitus, sicut dicitur ephe .5. (5:5),
hic dominum secum habet, et est cum domino per ueram caritatem. Qui
uero e contrario aliud quodcumque plus uel eque cum domino amat et

100 ueneratur: contra dominum est. *Nemo enim potest duobus dominis
servire,* scilicet sibi inuicem aduersantibus, sicut dicitur in Mt
.6. (6:24). Unde statim sequitur. Nemo enim potest *deo seruire et
mammone.*

II. Qui eciam non assumit *nomen dei in uanum* (Ex 20:7) id est,

105 qui non iurat falso nec superflue nec dolose nec sine causa, nec
honorem nominis domini dei evanescere facit male sentiendo de deo
secundum quamcumque heresim, nec fidem sine operibus putat sufficere
ad salutem quia *fides sine operibus mortua est,* sicut dicitur in

the contrary the mighty in evil will be the more mightily tested. Yes, we read in Wisdom 6 (6:9), 'over the mighty hangs a mightier menace.' The just also, through the justice 'which is everlasting and undying' (Wis 1:15), as we read in Wisdom 5 (5:16) 'are with the Lord and will live forever,' because as we read in Wisdom 3 (3:1) 'in the hand of the Lord are the souls of the just and the torment of evil will not touch them.' 'The unjust who perish,' however, are opposed to the Lord and therefore according to the psalm (36:38), 'together with them their posterity will be destroyed.' Those also who live moderately, 'who crucify their flesh with its passions and desires,' as we read in Galatians 5 (5:24), and as we read in Romans 13 (13:14), 'who by the spirit put to death the misdeeds of the body' are with the Lord, and therefore will live forever, according to Romans 8 (8:13). On the contrary, they who 'live according to the flesh,' will die forever, as we read in the same chapter (Rm 8:13). Such a life is forbidden in Sirach 18 (18:30–31), 'do not follow your base desires; that will make you the laughing-stock of your enemies.'

I. Just as we have touched briefly on the virtues, so also we must treat briefly of the commandments, for without them there is no salvation. Hence we read in Matthew 19 (19:16), 'if you would enter life, keep the commandments,' that is, of the decalogue. Therefore the person who adores only the triune God, who loves and venerates God above all others, without making for himself a graven or molten image or making for himself a god of his belly, for persons are said to exist, 'whose god is their belly,' as we read in Philippians 3 (3:19), 'their god is their belly,' without making idols of ephemeral things through avarice, because as we read in Ephesians 5 (5:5), 'avarice is enslavement to idols,' such a one has God with him and exists with the Lord through perfect love. On the contrary, one who loves and venerates anything whatever equally with or more than the Lord, is opposed to the Lord. 'No one can serve two masters,' who are mutual rivals, as we read in Matthew 6 (6:24). Hence this truth follows immediately: no one can 'serve both God and mammon.'

II. One who does not take the name of God in vain (Ex 20:7), that is, one who does not swear falsely, or unnecessarily, or deceitfully, or without cause, one who does not make the honor of the name of the Lord God vanish by having false ideas of God according to some heresy, and one who does not think that faith without works is sufficient for

Iacobo .2. (2:20): hic cum domino est, et cum domino ambulat profi-
110 ciendo, secundum illud Michee .6. (6:8) *Indicabo tibi o homo quid
sit tibi bonum*, (f. 74r) *et quid deus requirat a te, utique facere
iudicium, et diligere misericordiam et sollicitum ambulare cum deo
tuo.* Qui nomen dei aliquo predictorum modorum assumit in uanum,
contra dominum est. Unde in ecclesiastico .23. (23:10) dicitur.
115 *Nominatio dei non sit assidua in ore tuo*, et in eodem (23:9). *Iuracioni
non assuescat os tuum*, et in Mt .5. (5:34, 37) *Ego dico uobis
non omnino iurare: sed sit sermo uester est est, non non.* Et in
Iacobi ultimo, (5:12) *Ante omnia autem nolite iurare.* Suple nisi
necessarium fuerit tibi propter alios, et tunc per deum non per
120 aliud iurare, ne alicui ali rei diuinam reuerentiam exhibere credamini.
Quod autem in casu licitum sit uerum iurare: habetur in deuteronomio
.x. (10:20) ubi dicitur. *Dominum deum tuum timebis, et ei
seruies, ipsique adherebis, iurabisque in nomine illius.* Species
quoque male iurandi possunt sciri per hos uersus:

125   *Si male iurandi species sit cura notandi:*
        per primas fato, per idonea commemorato,

scilicet, per duas primas litteras huius uerbi fato: intelliguntur
duo iuramenta scilicet, per f: falsa iuracio, per a: appetitus
iurandi. Item per singulas litteras huius uerbi ydonea: intelliguntur
130 iuramenta peruersa: scilicet, per i: impetuosa iuracio, per d:
dolosa, per o: ociosa, per n: negligens, per e: erronea, per a:
assidua.
    III. Preter hec qui sabbatum sanctificat: cum domino est. Qui
uero non: contra dominum est. Hic uero notandum est quod preceptum
135 de sabbato figuratiuum est, quia figurat nostram dominicam, in qua
resurrexit dominus ad uitam eternam, que est requies eterna, sicut
quoque figurat sabbati, id est quietis diem ultimam, scilicet, diem
generalis resurrectionis, sed non cerimoniale,[13] quia secundum hebreum, illud est cerimoniale: cuius ratio ad litteram reddi non potest.
140 Ueniente autem ueritate: cessauit hoc mandatum quoad figuram,
quia *omnia in figura contingebant illis*, sicut dicitur ad cor .x.
(1 Co 10:11). In una tamen et eadem significacione dicitur sabbatum

salvation, since we read in James 2 (2:20), that 'faith without works is dead,' this person remains with the Lord and walks with the Lord by advancing according to Micah 6 (6:8): 'I will show you, O man, what is good for you and what God requires of you: of course, to do justice and to love mercy and to walk in awe with your God.' One who takes the name of God in any one of the preceding ways is opposed to the Lord. Hence we read in Sirach 23 (23:9–10) 'let no vain naming of God be habitually in your mouth,' and again, 'let not your mouth grow accustomed to oaths.' In Mt 5 (5:34, 37), 'but I say to you, do not swear at all . . . Let your words be "yes" or "no."' In the last chapter of James also we read: 'but above all do not swear' (5:12). Add: unless it be necessary for you to swear on account of others, and then swear by God and not by anything else, lest someone think you are showing divine reverence to some other. In this instance, we read in Deuteronomy 10 (10:20) that it is licit to swear to the truth, for there we read that 'you shall fear the Lord your God; you shall serve him and cleave to him, and you shall swear by his name.' The species of false oaths can be known through these verses:

> if you wish to keep in mind
> these false oaths of every kind,
> make the 'f' and 'a' of *fate*
> with *idonea* relate.

This means that with the first two letters of the word *fate*, two aspects of oaths are understood, namely, with the 'f' a false oath and with the 'a' an appetite for oaths. Likewise with the individual letters of the word *idonea*, different kinds of false oaths are meant, namely: with the 'i' an impetuous but with the 'd' a deceitful oath, with the 'o' an otiose but with the 'n' a negligent oath, with the 'e' an erroneous but with the 'a' an assiduous oath.

III. Moreover, one who keeps holy the sabbath, is with the Lord; one who does not, is opposed to the Lord. Now note here that the command about the Sabbath is figurative, because it prefigures our Sunday, when the Lord rose to eternal life, that is to eternal rest, just as it also prefigures the last day of Sabbath, that is of rest, namely, the day of general resurrection. It does not mean a ceremonial,[13] because according to the Hebrew, the meaning of a ceremonial can not be translated literally. With the advent of truth this command ceased to be a figure, because 'all happened to them in prefigurement,' as we read in Corinthians 10 (1 Co 10:11). With one and the same meaning, then, in the old testament the seventh day is called the

dies septimus in ueteri testamento, et dies octaua in nouo, scilicet,
dies quietis significatiua. Hoc tamen commune tunc restringebatur

145 ad aliud significandum, scilicet, diem septimam, nunc autem
ad aliud, scilicet, diem octauam. Hoc autem non facit aliud et
aliud preceptum simpliciter, nec aliquo modo nisi solum quoad hoc
quod tunc ad alium nunc autem ad alium diem restringitur. Ad hoc
eciam racionabiliter potest adici quod eciam quilibet dies septimane

150 ad alios comparatus unus dici potest. Mutacio ergo quietis hanc
facit mutacionem obseruacionis, quia patres ueteris legis septenarii,
sancti uero noui testamenti, octonarii sunt obseruatores propter
octavam resurrectionis dominice, et octauam resurrectionis future,
cuius silere non inuenitur in aliquo aliorum preceptorum, et

155 ideo illa non sunt mutata sicut hoc.

　　　IV. Qui eciam honorat *patrem et matrem* ut sit *longeuus super*
terram: (Deut 5:16) cum deo est qui hoc precipit; qui uero inhonorat
contra dominum est. Hoc primo exponatur de patre et matre corporali
ad litteram quos honorare debemus necessaria si indigeant

160 ministrando. Unde dicitur in ecclesiastico .3. (3:8). *Qui timet*
dominum honorat parentes, et quasi dominis seruiet hiis qui se genuerunt,
et in prouerbiis .28. (28:24). *Qui subtrahit aliquid a pa-*
tre et matre et dicit hoc (f. 74v) non est peccatum: particeps est

[ima pagina,	*ydola sperne - dei nomen tibi non sit inane.*
f. 74v,	*Sabbata sanctifices. Habeas in honore parentes.*
eadem manu]	*Non occisor eris, mechus, fur, testis iniquus.*
	Non aliam nuptas, non res cupias alienas.

165 *homicide.* Et in Mt .15. *uos transgredimini mandata dei propter*
traditionem uestram (15:3). Ubi dicitur in textu. *Uos autem dicitis.*
Quicumque dixerit patri aut matri munus quodcumque est ex me
tibi proderit (15:5 - interlin. scilicet, sicut mihi), et non honorificauerit
patrem suum aut matrem suam, suple benefecit, uel uita

170 eterna dignus est, *et irritum fecistis mandatum dei* scilicet de honore
parentum: in exodus .xx. (20:12). (scriptum super *honorificauerit*
interlin.: uel interrogative est; marg. est proderit ipsorum?

Sabbath and in the new the eighth day is called the Sabbath, namely, the day which means rest. But this meaning common to both, was restricted to one meaning then, namely, the seventh day, and to another meaning now, namely, the eighth day. But this does not add one precept to another absolutely, nor in any other way but in this only, that the day of rest was then restricted to one day but now to another. To this also can be reasonably added, that any day falling on the seventh day by comparison with others, can be called the first day. Therefore the change of the day of rest brings about this change in observance, because the fathers of the old law were observers of the seventh day, while the saints of the new testament are observers of the octave, because the Lord's resurrection was on the eight day and the future resurrection will be on the eighth day. Such an omission is not found in any one of the other precepts and therefore the other precepts have not been changed as this has.

IV. One who honors father and mother and so will be long-lived upon earth (Dt 5:16), is also with God, who gave this precept; but one who dishonors parents, is opposed to God. According to the letter, this is proclaimed primarily of one's father and mother in the flesh, whom we must honor by providing what is needed if they are in want. Hence we read in Sirach 3 (3:8), 'one who fears the Lord, honors his parents, and will serve his parents as his masters,' and in Proverbs 28 (28:24), 'one who robs father or mother and says (f. 74v) "this is no transgression",

[At the bottom of f. 74r in the same hand, the ten commandments in verse:]

> No idol choose; revere God's holy name;
> The sabbath hallow; love your parents both;
> Don't kill or lust or steal or swear false oath;
> Desire no other's spouse, no other's claim.

shares in homicide.' In Matthew (15:3) we read: 'you transgress the commands of God for the sake of your tradition,' where we read in the text (Mt 15:5), 'but you claim that one who says to father or mother, whatever blessing comes from me will benefit you,' [interlined: just as it does me], 'and does not honor his father,' add: has done well, or is worthy of eternal life, 'and you have made void the commandment of God,' namely, about honoring parents, according to Exodus 20 (20:12). [Interlined: or this is an interrogative; in margin: about 5 illegible words.]

qui? d?). Tenemur eciam honorare patrem et matrem spiritualem,
scilicet, christum, et eos qui in eius loco sunt constituti, scilicet,
175 prelatos et ecclesiam. Unde dicitur in .1. thimothei .5. (5:17).
Qui bene presunt: duplici honore digni sunt, et in Regum .24. (1 S
24:7). *Propicius sit mihi dominus ne faciam hanc rem domino meo
christo domini ut mittam manum in eum: quoniam christus domini est.*
Obseruatoribus eciam huius precepti premium promittitur, cum sit
180 preceptum primum secunde tabule magis quam obseruatoribus aliorum
similiter ad proximos pertinencium, ut quod in primo promissum est:
et in aliis seruatis speretur. Uel quia hoc solum in secunda tabula
est directe preceptum, alia tamen omnia sint prohibiciones, ad quas
potest proprie dici si hiis uel hiis non feceris: hiis uel hiis penam
185 non sustinebis. Non enim sufficit ad uitam eternam abstinere a
malo: nisi eciam bona fiant. Unde in psalmo (36: 27) dicitur. *Declina
a malo et fac bonum* etc. Et in ysaia .1. (1:17). *Quiescite
agere peruerse, discite benefacere.* Mater quoque ecclesia honoratur,
quando communis utilitas priuate preponitur. *Caritas enim non
190 querit que sua sunt,* sicut dicitur corinthiis .13. (1 Co 13:5).
Honoratur eciam christus in suis et ecclesia in temporalium collacione.
Unde dicitur in prouerbiis .3. (3:9) *Honora dominum de tua
substancia, et de primiciis frugum tuarum da pauperibus.* Honoratur
quoque in spiritualibus, scilicet, per doctrinam uerbi dei. Dicitur
195 enim in .1. cor .ix. (9:11). *Si seminauerimus uobis spiritualia
parum* est *si uestra carnalia metamus.* Hanc matrem uestram christus
uerus sponsus sibi desponsauit dum pro ea se morti exposuit. *Sponsa
enim nubit: dum sponsus moritur,* sicut dicit augustinus. De quibus,
scilicet, sponso et sponsa habetur in io .3. (3:29) *Qui habet sponsam:
200 sponsus est.* Qui igitur honorat patrem et matrem: *uita uiuet
longiore,* sicut dicitur in ecclesiastico .3. (3:7), hoc est *honora
patrem et matrem ut sis longeuus super terram,* scilicet, uiuencium,
id est, ut eternaliter uiuas. Quod autem qui inhonorat patrem et
matrem sit contra dominum: patet per illud ecclesiastici .3.
205 (3:18). *Quam male fame est qui relinquit patrem, et est maledictus
a deo: qui exas perat matrem,* et in eodem (3:13). *Gloria hominis ex
honore patris sui, et dedecus filii: pater sine honore,* et in eodem
(3:11). *Benedictio patris firmat domos filiorum, maledictio autem
matris eradicat fundamenta.*

197–98. Citationem augustinianam non inveni.

We are also bound to honor our spiritual father and mother, namely Christ and those who have been appointed in his place, namely the prelates and the church. Hence we read in 1 Timothy 5 (5:17), 'those who preside well are worthy of double honor,' and in 1 Samuel 24 (24:7) 'may the Lord preserve me from doing such a thing to my lord and raising my hand against him, for he is the Lord's anointed.' Since this is the first precept of the second tablet, a reward is promised to those who observe it, rather than to those who observe the other precepts, which likewise refer to our neighbors, that what is promised in the first may be hoped for in observing the rest. Or perhaps because in the second tablet this only is a direst command, while all the rest are prohibitions regarding which it can be properly said, that if you have not acted in this way or that, you will not suffer the penalty for this or that. It is not sufficient for eternal life that you abstain from evil, unless you also perform good deeds. Therefore we read in the psalm (37:27): 'turn away from evil and do good,' etc., and in Isaiah 1 (1:17) 'cease doing evil, learn to do good.'

Mother Church is also honored, when the common good is placed before the private good, because according to 1 Corinthians 13 (13:5), 'perfect love does not seek what belongs to itself.' Christ is honored in his members and in the Church by the offering of temporal goods. Hence we read in Proverbs 3 (3:9), 'honor the Lord from your substance, and from your first-fruits give alms to the poor.' The Lord is also honored in spiritual goods, namely, through the teaching of the word of God. We read in 1 Corinthians 9 (9:11), 'if we have sown spiritual goods among you,' it is a slight matter, 'if we reap your corporal blessings.' This mother of yours, Christ the true spouse took as his bride, while he offered himself to death for her. As Augustine says, 'the bride is wed, while the groom's blood is shed.' About the Bridegroom and his bride we read in John 3 (3:29), 'he who has the bride is the Bridegroom.' Therefore, one who honors father and mother, 'will live a longer life,' as we read in Sirach 3 (3:7); that is, 'honor your father and mother, that you may be long-lived, in the land of the living,' that is, that you may live eternally. But that anyone who dishonors father or mother is opposed to the Lord, is evident from the verse of Sirach 3 (3:18), 'of what ill repute is one who forsakes a father! And anyone who provokes a mother is cursed by God.' In the same chapter (3:13), 'a person's glory derives from honoring a father and a child's disgrace is a father without honor.' In the same chapter (3:11), 'a father's blessing strengthens the homes of children but a mother's curse overturns their foundations.'

210   V. Qui eciam non occidit: quoad hoc cum domino est. Qui uero
occidit: contra dominum est, igitur non occides, scilicet, occisione
sequente iram, quod non facit iudex. Occidit autem quis alium
multipliciter. Primo: manu. Unde dicitur in Genesi .9. (9:6). *Quicumque effuderit sanguinem humanum: fundetur sanguis ipsius.* Secundo:

215   mente. Unde dicitur .1. Ioanne .3. (3:15). *Qui odit fratrem
suum: homicida est.* Tercio: subtrahendo auxilium uite, et hoc uel
corporaliter uel spiritualiter. Unde ambrosius. *Pasce fame morientem,
quod si non paueris: occidisti.* Et est intelligendus (f. 75r)
de utroque pastu, scilicet, corporali et spirituali. Similiter

220   eciam quod dicitur in iohanne ultimo (21:16–17). *Pasce, pasce,
pasce,* de utroque pastu intelligi debet. Quarto: uerbo uel exemplo.
Unde in Leuitico .xix. (19:14). *Non maledices surdo, nec coram ceco
ponas offendiculum.* Quinto, scandalizando. Unde in Mt .18. (18:6)
dicitur. *Qui scandalizauerit unum de pusillis istis qui in me credunt:*

225   *expedit ei ut mola asinaria suspendatur in collo eius, et
demergatur in profundum inferni.* Quod autem qui occidit est contra
dominum: patet per hoc quod dicitur in .1. Io .3. (3:15). *Scitis
quoniam omnis homicida non habet uitam eternam in se manentem* et
ita nec dominum, et sic non est cum domino, sed contra dominum.

230   VI. Similiter et qui non mechatur, quantum ad hoc: cum domino
est. Qui uero mechatur: contra dominum. Igitur *non mechaberis*,
(Deut 5:18). Sciendum uero est quoniam hoc nomine mechie omnis
illicitus concubitus prohibetur, scilicet omnis quicumque fieri solet
extra legitimum matrimonium. Committitur uero luxuria actualiter

235   primo, sicut tangitur in prouerbiis .6. (6:30) *Non grandis est
culpa cum quis furatur, furatur enim ut esurientem impleat animam.
Qui autem adulter est propter cordis inopiam: perdet animam suam*
(6:32). Secundo: mente secundum illud Mt.5. (5:28). *Qui uiderit
mulierem ad concupiscendum eam, iam mechatus est in corde suo.*

240   Tercio: coeundo cum alienigenis. Unde dicitur in Hesdra .9. (2 Esd
9:2). Contraxerunt filii israel cum alienigenis contra domini pro-
hibicionem, scilicet, in deu .vii. (7:2–3) ubi dicitur. *Non inibis
cum eis fedus, nec misereberis earum, neque sociabis cum eis coniuga.*
Quod autem luxuriosi sunt contra dominum: planum est, quia

245   *neque fornicarii neque adulteri regnum dei possidebunt*, sicut dicitur
.1. cor .6. (6:9–10).

217–18. Ambrosius, PL 15: 1881A.

V. One who does not kill, thus far is also with the Lord; but one who kills is opposed to the Lord. Therefore you shall not kill, namely, with a killing that follows anger, which is not the act of a judge. But one person kills another in many ways. First by hand. Hence we read in Genesis 9 (9:6), 'one who sheds the blood of man, by man shall have his blood shed.' Second, mentally. Hence we read in 1 John 3 (3:15), 'anyone who hates his brother is a murderer.' Third, by withdrawing an aid to life, and this either corporally or spiritually. Hence Ambrose says: 'feed a man dying of hunger, for if you do not feed him, you have killed him.' And his word is to be understood (f. 75r) of both nourishments, namely, for both body and spirit. Likewise the words in the last chapter of John, 'feed . . . feed . . . feed' (21:16–17), should be understood of both kinds of nourishment. Fourth, by word or example. Hence we read in Leviticus 19 (19:14) 'you shall not curse the deaf, nor put a stumblingblock before the blind.' Fifth, by scandal. We read in Matthew 18 (18:6), 'whoever scandalizes one of these little ones who believe in me, would be better drowned in the depths of the pit with a millstone hung from his neck.' That he who kills is opposed to the Lord is clear from what is said in 1 John 3 (3:15), 'you know that a murderer has neither eternal life abiding in him,' nor the Lord abiding in him. So he is not with the Lord but opposed to the Lord.

VI. Likewise, one who does not commit adultery, to this extent is with the Lord; but one who commits adultery is opposed to the Lord. Therefore, 'you shall not commit adultery' (Dt 5:18). Now you should know that by the word adultery is forbidden all unlawful promiscuity, that is, any and every act wont to be committed outside legitimate matrimony. First, lust is committed in action and is treated in Proverbs 6 (6:30, 32): 'when one steals, the guilt is not great, for one steals to fill a starving life,' 'but one who is an adulterer for his heart's need, will lose his life.' Secondly, in thought, according to the verse in Matthew 5 (5:28), 'if a man looks at a woman lustfully, he has already committed adultery with her in his heart.' Thirdly, by intercourse with foreigners. Hence we read in Ezra 9 (2 Esd 9:2), that the children of Israel intermarried with foreigners contrary to the Lord's prohibition, namely, in Deuteronomy 7 (7:2–3), 'you shall make no covenant with them, nor show mercy to them, nor marry them.' That the lustful are opposed to the Lord is obvious, because 'neither fornicators nor adulterers will possess the kingdom of God,' as we read in 1 Corinthians 6 (6:9–10).

VII. Qui eciam furtum non facit quoad hoc: cum domino est. Qui
autem furatur: contra dominum est. Fit autem furtum primo ad litteram. Et secundum hoc: furtum est omnis attrectacio rei aliene inuito
250   domino, ut dicitur in Glossa. Unde super illud, *non furtum*
facies: talis est interlinearis: *quamlibet rei usurpacionem quod*
uicium est rapacitatis. Unde dicitur in Thobia .2. (2:21) *Non licet*
nobis aut edere ex furto aliquid aut contingere. Secundo: spiritualiter,
ut in malis prelatis. Unde in Io .x. (10:10) dicitur.
255   *Fur non uenit nisi ut furetur et mactet et perdat.* Tercio: per
seductionem hereticam, sicut dicitur in prouerbiis .9. (9:17). *Aque*
furtiue dulciores sunt, et panis absconditus suauior. Quia uero
neque fures neque auari, neque ebriosi regnum dei possidebunt, sicut
dicitur .1. cor .6. (6:10): patet quod qui furtum committunt:
260   contra dominum sunt.

VIII. Qui eciam non loquitur contra proximum falsum testimonium: cum domino est, quoad hoc. Qui autem hoc facit: contra dominum. Si uero queritur qualiter hoc preceptum a secundo prime tabule
differat: respondendum est, quia illud proprie ad dominum, illud ad
265   proximum pertinet. Unde ibi dicitur. *Non assumes nomen dei tui in*
uanum. Hic autem *non loqueris contra proximum tuum falsum testimo-*
nium. Preterea illud in iurando, hoc autem in simpliciter asserendo
multociens consistit. In hoc eciam precepto et actus mendacii et
uoluntas prohiberi creduntur. Unde dicitur in ecclesiastico .7.
270   (7:14). *Noli uelle mentiri omne mendacium.* Quod autem mentientes
contra dominum sunt: patet per illud ps .5. (5:7). *Perdes omnes qui*
locuntur mendacium, et sapientia .1. (1:11). *Os quod mentitur*
occidit animam, et in prouerbiis .19. (19:5). *Falsus testis non*
erit impunitus.
275   IX. Qui eciam non concupiscit domum proximi sui: in hoc cum
domino; qui autem concupiscit contra dominum est. Huic autem con-
trarium uidetur quod dicitur, quod *lex cohibet manum non animum.*
Preterea non posset (f. 75v) secundum legem puniri concupiscens,

---

278   ⎧ *in domino, non in seculo,*
[ima pagina   ⎨ *in ueritate, non in iniquitate,*
f.75v]   *gaudete*   ⎩ *in spe eternitatis, non in flore uanitatis.*

---

250. quod *in glossa* non inueni. 251–52. quod *in interlineari* nec inueni.

VII. One who does not steal, to this extent is with the Lord; but one who steals is opposed to the Lord. First of all theft is committed literally, and in this way, as we read in the gloss, theft is any filching of another's possession without the owner's consent. Hence, on this verse, 'you shall not steal,' the interlinear defines theft as 'any usurpation of a possession, which is the vice of greed.' Hence as we read in Tobit 2 (2:21), 'we have no right to eat or even to touch stolen goods.' Second, spiritually, as among bad prelates. Hence we read in John 10 (10:10), 'the thief comes only to steal, to kill and to destroy.' Thirdly, through the seduction of heresy, as we read in Proverbs 9 (9:17), 'stolen waters are sweeter and bread eaten secretly is tastier.' But because 'neither thieves, nor the greedy, nor drunkards . . . will possess the kingdom of God,' as we read in 1 Corinthians 6 (6:10) clearly those who commit theft are opposed to the Lord.

VIII. One who does not speak false witness against his neighbor, to this extent is with the Lord; but one who so speaks, is opposed to the Lord. If you ask, however, to what degree this precept differs from the second precept of the first tablet, one must answer that the former refers properly to the Lord, the latter to one's neighbor. So there we read: 'you shall not take the name of your God in vain,' but here: 'you shall not speak false witness against your neighbor.' Moreover, the former most often consists in taking an oath, but the latter most often simply in making a statement. In the present precept the act of lying and the will to lie are also believed to be forbidden. Hence we read in Sirach 7 (7:14), 'be loth to tell lies at all.' That liars are opposed to the Lord, is clear from a verse of Psalm 5 (5:7), 'you will destroy all who speak falsehood,' and in Wisdom 1 (1:11) 'a lying mouth deals death to the soul,' and in Proverbs 19 (19:5) 'a false witness will not go unpunished.'

IX. One who does not covet his neighbor's house, in this also is with the Lord; but one who covets is opposed to the Lord. An aphorism seems to contradict this precept: namely, that 'law checks the hand, not the spirit.' Moreover (f. 75v) the covetous could not be punished accord-

[at the foot of folio 75r in rime are these reasons for rejoicing:]

Rejoice {
in the Lord, not in the world,
in the truth, not in wickedness,
in hope of eternity, not in the blossom of vanity.

scilicet, quia *nec sciri posset concupiscentis concupiscentia.* Re-
280 spondendum est. Hoc preceptum est sequens illud de furto, et quasi
scilicet, quia *nec sciri posset concupiscentis concupiscentia.* Re-
280 spondendum est. Hoc preceptum est sequens illud de furto, et quasi
coniungens precepta legis cum euangelio, in quo expresse dampnatur
concupiscentia, ut in Mt .5. (5:28). *Qui uiderit mulierem,* etc. Hec
autem precepta sic sunt intelligenda, non concupisces uel desiderabis,
etc., id est, nullum signum concupiscentie uel desiderii os-
285 tendes. In nouo autem testamento eciam concupiscentia prohibetur
interior. *Non ergo concupisces domum proximi tui* (Ex 20:17). Unde
dicitur in ysaia .5. (5:8). *Ve qui coniungitis domum ad domum,* etc.
    X. Qui eciam uxorem proximi non concupiscit: cum domino est.
quoad hoc. Qui autem desiderat contra dominum est. Hoc autem pro-
290 hibitum est a domino, in ecclesiastico .9. (9:12), ubi dicitur. *Cum*
aliena muliere non sedeas, etc. Quod autem dicitur non seruum non
ancillam: ad nonum preceptum magis uidentur pertinere, quam ad decimum. Ad quod potest dici quod qui uxorem proximi concupiscit: et
contra nonum et contra decimum peccat, scilicet, quia contra legem
295 matrimonii et contra possessionem proximi peccat, quia eciam uxor
in possessionibus uiri est, et ideo potuit in utroque poni prohibicio
de concupiscentia uxoris. Quod igitur huius precepti trans-
gressores contra dominum sunt: patet per premissa. De hiis enim
dicit Ysidorus. *Primum mandatum probibet subreptionem. Secundum:*
300 *errorem. Tercium: seculi interficit amorem. Quartum impietatem.*
Quintum crudelitatem. Sextum fornicacionem. Septimum rapacitatem.
Octauum perimit falsitatem. Nonum: mundi cupiditatem. Decimum:
adulterii cogitacionem. Et notandum est quod sicut .x. plagis per-
cuciuntur egyptii: .x. preceptis scribuntur tabule ut populus regatur
305 *et demones occidantur.* Unde Augustinus de decacordo psalterio
Tange primam cordam: et cecidit bestia supersticionis. Tange secundam:
et cecidit bestia erroris nefandarum heresium. Tange terciam
et cecidit bestia crudelior, scilicet, amor mundi, per quem tantum
laborant homines. Tange quartam: et cecidit bestia impietatis.
310 *Tange quintam: et cecidit bestia libidinis. Tange sextam: et*

299–305. *glossa,* PL 114:254C; 458:CD. 306–317. PL 38:67, 75a; 75b; 46:945–954.

ing to the law. Why? Because the 'covetousness of the covetous could not be detected.' The reply should be: this precept follows the one on theft and as it were, links the precepts of the law with the gospel, in which covetousness is expressly condemned, as in Matthew 5 (5:28), 'a man who looks at a woman,' etc. But these precepts should be understood as follows: you shall not covet nor desire, etc., that is, you shall show no sign of covetousness or desire. But in the new testament even interior covetousness is prohibited. 'Therefore you shall not covet your neighbor's house' (Ex 20:17). Hence we read in Isaiah 5 (5:8), 'woe to you who join house to house,' etc.

X. One who does not covet his neighbor's wife, to this extent also is with the Lord, but one who covets is opposed to the Lord. This is forbidden by the Lord in Sirach 9 (9:12), where we read: never sit down with another's wife,' etc. But because neither slave nor handmaid is mentioned here, both seem to belong to the ninth rather than the tenth commandment. In reply it can be said that one who covets his neighbor's wife, sins against both the ninth and the tenth commandments, because he sins against both the law of matrimony and a possession of his neighbor, since even a wife belongs with the posessions of a husband, and therefore the prohibition against coveting a wife can be listed under both commandments. From what precedes, therefore, it is clear that those who transgress this commandment are opposed to the Lord.

Isidore writes this about the commandments: 'the first commandment prohibits deception; the second, error. The third kills love for the world, the fourth, impiety; the fifth, cruelty; the sixth, fornication; the seventh, greed. The eighth forbids falsehood; the ninth, covetousness of the world; the tenth, the thought of adultery. And note that as the Egyptians were stricken with the ten plagues, so the tablets were inscribed with the ten precepts, that the people might be governed and the demons slain.'

Therefore Augustine writes of the ten-stringed harp. 'Touch the first string and there falls the beast of superstition; touch the second, and then falls the beast of the error of accursed heresies. Touch the third and there falls a beast more cruel, namely the love of the world through which people endure such travail; touch the fourth and then falls the beast of impiety. Touch the fifth and there falls the beast of lust; touch the sixth and

cecidit bestia crudelitatis. Tange septimam: et cecidit bestia
rapacitatis. Tange octavam: et cecidit bestia falsitatis. Tange
nonam: et cecidit bestia adulterine cogitacionis. Tange decimam: et
cecidit bestia cupiditatis. Sic patet per .x. cordas .x. precepta
315 *decalogi significari. Hee autem bestie significantur per .x. cornua*
bestie terribilis et fortis et reliqua suis pedibus conculcantis,
diaboli, scilicet, uel antichristi, in daniel .7. (7:7). Nos igitur
qui nichil boni ex nobis habere possumus dominum humiliter deprece-
mur ut ipse qui potest det nobis per caritatem et alias uirtutes et
320 decalogi obseruacionem ei adherere, et cum ipso in presenti esse,
ut ipse per misericordiam suam nos secum ducat ad eternam beatitudinem, quam ipse prestare dignetur, etc.

[323 f. 75v, ima pagina] Gregorius: Nullum sacrificium adeo placet: sicut zelus animarum
(PL 76:932C). Chrysostom: Oracio iugis infirmitas est hostis: ceterum ipse contra se tela
ministrat, qui hostem precum instancia non fatigat (quod nondum inveni).

then falls the beast of cruelty. Touch the seventh and there falls the beast of greed; touch the eighth and then falls the beast of falsehood. Touch the ninth and there falls the beast of wanton thoughts; touch the tenth and then falls the beast of cupidity. Thus by the ten strings are obviously meant the ten commandments. But these beasts are meant by the ten horns of the terrifying and powerful beast, who tramples all else beneath his hoofs, that is, the devil or the antichrist of Daniel 7, (Dn 7:7). Therefore, we who can derive no good from ourselves, beseech the Lord, that he who has the power, may in charity allow us to offer him not only the other virtues but also the observance of the decalogue, and in the present life to dwell with him, that through his mercy he may take us with him to the eternal happiness which he has deigned to offer, and so forth.

[At the foot of f. 75v:] Gregory: No sacrifice pleases as much as zeal for souls. Chrysostom: Incessant prayer weakens the enemy; in brief, one who does not weaken the enemy with incessant prayer, supplies weapons against himself.

VI.   THE GREAT SUPPER

1. B.M. SLOANE 2478 The great supper means the eternal refreshment in happiness of the saved. 2. The net of the church or of evangelization hauls in both good fish and bad to be separated at the end like wheat and weeds, grain and chaff, sheep and goats. 3. This happiness is unending. 4. The supper like a wedding, attracts wise and foolish, those with and those without the wedding garment of prayer and merit. 5. The supper is called great for many reasons: because of the number of guests and 6. the greatness of saints and angels, with no small fish caught in the net; 7. because of the number and delicacy of the courses served, for 'all earthly and heavenly blessings will be openly and obviously present;' 8. because of the duration, 'for we shall rest and gaze and love and praise' forever; 9. since all are invited, for many are called to the faith though few are chosen for the kingdom; 10. because today God calls in many ways: through words, blessings and curses, inner inspirations, the law, the prophets and the ministry of preachers. 11. We read of the triple invitation and 12. of the threefold excuses, for those who would share the bread of the kingdom must be really good, not addicted to earthly goods, idle curiosity or the pleasures of this world. Ambrose and Bede interpret the three classes, who reject the invitation. 14. In the second invitation the poor are introduced: the weak, the blind, the lame; both groups: those who excused themselves and those introduced, were sinners; the first were invited and the last compelled; but what else is misfortune but compulsion? Many guests gather for the supper from among the Jews, but space remains to accomodate a great many Gentiles, and the number must be completed for the final summons.

VI. LONDON, B.M., SLOANE MS 2478, *ff.* 82R–83V

(1) Sermo Magistri Serlonis (dominica secunda post pentecosten) *Homo quidem fecit cenam magnam* etc. Lucas .14. (14:16). Notandum quod sicut dicit Beda in glossa, *Hoc prandium non prandium sed cena dicitur. Sed quia post prandium: de quo Mt. agit 22. (22:1–14) cena*

5 *restat. Post cenam: nullum conuiuium restat. De prandio: multi. De cena: nullus eicitur.* Per hunc (Bedam) in glossa, aperte intelligitur quod per prandium de quo agit Mt: significatur refectio ecclesie militantis, quoniam congregauerunt modo boni et mali. Sed in fine mali expellentur ad fines infernales, sicut manifeste intelligitur

10 per illum non uestitum ueste nuptiali, qui expulsus erat ligatis manibus et pedibus in tenebras exteriores (Mt 22:11). Boni ad gloriam introducentur. Per cenam uero significatur eterna refectio in eterna beatitudine, ad quam introibunt soli saluandi, et inde nullus expelletur.

15 (2) Hic eciam boni significantur Mt .13. (47–48) ubi dicitur. *Simile est regnum celorum sagene misse in mare et ex omni genere piscium congreganti, quam cum impleta esset, educantes et secus litus sedentes elegerunt bonos in uasa sua, malos autem foras miserunt.* Unde dicit Gregorius in glossa quod sagene comparatur presens

20 ecclesia uel predicacio euangelica que a fluentibus seculi ad celum trahit. Secundo eciam dicit quod piscatores spirituales, scilicet, apostoli et eorum sequentes *contexerunt sibi sagenam ex ueteri et nouo testamento, quam miserunt in mare huius seculi, que usque hodie trahitur in fluctibus capiens quicquid incidit bonos et malos,*

25 *quos ad litus trahit,* id est, ad finem mundi, ut tunc *fiat diuisio saluandorum a dampnandis* et granorum *a paleis,* Mt .3.(3:12) tritici a zizannia (sic), Mt .13. (13:30), ouium ab hedis, Mt .25. (25:33).

(3) Huius ergo cene factio eterne beatitudinis est prouisio et preparacio, ut super illud, Mt .25. (25:34) *uenite benedicti patris*

30 *mei, possidete regnum quod uobis preparatum est a constitutione mundi.* Dicitur in interlineari: *beneficio patris mei promoti ad*

3–6. *Glossa,* PL 114:308C, *Beda, idem* 92:514B, *Gregorius* I, 76:1267AB. 19. *Gregorius in glossa* non inveni. 23. 'Ista est sagena quae in mare hujus saeculi mittitur.' Hieronymus, P.L. 25:307C. 27. Greg. 76:1116BC, glossa, 114:133D–134A. 31–33. Dicitur in *interlineari,* i.e. in Glossa 114:166B.

VI. *A Sermon of Master Serlo (for the Second Sunday after Pentecost)*

B. M. SLOANE, MS 2478

(1) 'A man once gave a great supper,' etc. (Lk 14:16). Notice that as Bede says in the gloss: 'this is not called a dinner but a supper. Yes, because after the dinner of which Matthew treats in chapter 22 (22:1–14), there remains a supper. After supper no guest remains, but after dinner many remain.' Through Bede in the gloss, it is clearly understood that the dinner of which Matthew treats, means the refreshment of the church militant, because both good and bad are now assembled together. But in the end the bad will be expelled to the lower realms, which is the obvious meaning of that guest not dressed in wedding clothes. Bound hand and foot, he was cast into exterior darkness (Mt 22:11). But the good are introduced into glory. By the supper is meant eternal refreshment in everlasting happiness, to which only those destined to be saved will be introduced and from which no one will be expelled.

(2) The good are also meant here in Matthew 13 (13:47–48), where we read: 'the kingdom of heaven is like a drag-net cast into the sea to catch fish of every kind. When the net is full, the fishermen haul it ashore. Seated by the shore, they select the good fish for their baskets but toss aside the bad.' Hence in the gloss Gregory says that the present church or the heralding of the gospel is compared to a net, which hauls fish to heaven from the torrents of the world. Secondly, he says that spiritual fishermen, namely the apostle and their successors, 'from the old and the new testaments have woven a net for themselves, which they have cast into the sea of this world. Even to our day this net is towed through the waves to catch whatever swims by, good or bad. These the net hauls to shore,' that is, until the end of the world, that then 'may take place the separation of the saved from the damned, the grains from the chaff, Matthew 3 (3:12), wheat from weeds, Matthew 13 (13:30), sheep from goats, Matthew 25 (25:33).

(3) Hence preparation for this supper is the provision and preparation for eternal happiness, as in Matthew 25 (25:34), 'come blessed of my Father, inherit the kingdom prepared for you from the foundation of the world.' We read in the interlinear: 'by the blessing of my Father you

optinendam gloriam in qua sine corruptione regnetis ad quam predestinati
essetis a constitutione mundi (Mt 13:35).

(4) Hec eciam cena alibi nomine nupciarum appellatur. Et notan-

35 dum quod sicut nullus ab hac cena siue ab hiis nuptiis expellitur
qui semel fuerit ingressus: sic nullus ad has admittitur, nisi qui
paratus in aduentu sponsi inuenitur. Unde Mt. 25. legitur quod sa-
pientes uirgines *que parate erant ueniente sponso: intrauerunt cum*
eo ad nupcias et clausa est ianua. Relique uero, id est, fatue virgines

40 *per quas significantur reprobi: clamantes postea, domine, domine,*
aperi nobis, audierunt a domino, *amen dico uobis nescio uos*
(25:11–12). Ubi dicitur in interlineari. *Ideo uos desero, quia per*
uite meritum non cognosco, super quod dicit Gregorius: *O si sapere*
in cordis palato posset aliquis quid admiracionis habent quod dicitur,

45 *'ecce sponsus uenit;' quid dulcedinis: 'intrauerunt cum eo ad*
nupcias;' quid amaritudinis: 'clausa est ianua.' Et Augustinus dicit
quod *post iudicium non patet precum aut meritorum locucio* [Aug.
uero *locus*] secundum illud prouerbiorum .6. *zelus et furor viri non*
parcet in die uindicte (6:34) id est iudicii, *nec adquiescet cuius-*

50 *quam precibus, nec accipiet pro redemptione dona plurima* (6:35).

(5) *Fecit cenam magnam* etc. (Lc 14:16). Ex premissis satis patere
potest que sit hec cena et quare hec cena dicatur. Nunc restat
exponere quare dicatur magna. Uere igitur potest hec cena dici
magna, tum propter multitudinem cenancium, tum propter magnitudinem

55 eorumdem, tum propter apponendorum multitudinem, tum propter
eorumdem preciositatem, (f. 82v) tum eciam propter duracionis illius
perpetuitatem. Erunt enim multi in hac cena. Omnes igitur ad uitam
preordinati sunt ab inicio usque ad finem seculi, sicut dicitur ad
thessalonicenses .4. (4:17). *Mortui qui in christo sunt resurgent*

60 *primi,* etc. Et est sic intelligendum quod apostolus dixit, *nos qui*
uiuimus, etc. connumerando se cum aliis, quia tunc uiui inuenientur,
quia omnes sancti unum corpus christi et ecclesie sunt. Quod ait
eciam, *sic semper cum domino erimus* nonne intelligendum est quod
sancti semper sint mansuri cum domino in aere, sed *sic,* id est,

65 habentes corpora sempiterna, semper cum domino erimus? Ibi dicitur
in glossa, quod habent omnes anime cum a seculo exierunt diuersas

---

42. *Inter.* i.e. Greg. 76:1121D. 43. *Greg.* 76:1120C. 46–48. *Augustinus* et *Glossa*
114:305A, non *locutio* at *locus*. 66. *Glossa*, non inveni.

have been advanced to the possession of glory, in which you will reign without faltering, to which you have been predestined from the foundation of the world' (Mt 13:35).

(4) Elsewhere this supper is also called a wedding. Notice that just as no one who has once entered is excluded from this supper or from the wedding, so no one is admitted unless he is found ready at the coming of the bridegroom. In Mt 25 (25:11–12), we read that the wise virgins 'who were ready at the arrival of the bridegroom went in to the wedding with him, and the door was shut. But the rest, foolish virgins, through whom are meant the rejected, later shouted: "Lord, Lord, open for us." But they heard the Lord answer: "Amen, I say to you, I do not know you."' Here we read in the interlinear: 'I abandon you, because I do not know you through the merits of your life.' On this Gregory comments: 'if only one could taste with the palate of the heart what wonders lie in these words: "behold, the Bridegroom comes!" and what sweetness in these words: "they went in to the wedding hall with him!" but also what bitterness is in the words: "and the door was shut!"' Augustine comments that 'after the judgment no place remains for prayers or merits.' According to Proverbs 6 (6:34) 'a husband is never more angry than when he is jealous; he will not spare in the day of revenge,' that is, in the day of judgment. 'He will not accede to anyone's prayers, nor will he accept gifts in abundance for ransom' (Pr 6:35).

(5) 'He prepared a great supper,' etc. (Lk 14:16). From the preceding can be seen both what the supper is and why it is called a supper. It remains to explain why the supper is called great. This supper really can be called great, first from the great number of the guests, then from their distinction, thirdly from the number of courses and from their delicacy, and finally from the endless renewal of the supper. Many indeed will be the banqueters. All have been preordained for life from the beginning to the end of the world, as we read in 1 Thessalonians 4 (4:16–17). 'The dead who are in Christ will be the first to rise,' etc. In this way also should the words of the apostle be understood: 'then we who are still alive' etc., including himself with others, because then they shall be found alive, since all the saints are the one body of Christ and his Church. Should not Paul's statement, that 'thus we will always be with the Lord,' be also understood to mean that the saints will always remain with the Lord, 'in the air,' that is, have everlasting bodies, in such a way that we will always be with the Lord? There we read in the gloss, that all souls when they depart from this world have different welcomes: joy for the good torment for the evil. But when the resurrection of the saints

recepciones, habent gaudium bone, tormenta male. Sed cum sancta
fuerit resurrectio et bonorum gaudium amplius erit et malorum tormenta grauiora, quum cum corpore torquebuntur per illud Mt .25.
70 (25:34) *et tunc dicet eis qui a dextris* etc., dicitur in interlineari, *qui ad beatitudinem pertinentes soli.*
      (6) In hac eciam cena cum saluandis hominibus erunt illi ineffabiles
exercitus. ix. ordinum angelorum, quia tunc, scilicet, omnes
sancti sicut angeli erunt, sicut dicitur Mt .22. (22:30). Magni
75 eciam conuiue huius cene, quia illic non poterit esse paruus, scilicet,
quod significatur in magna captura piscium, Io .21. ubi cissum
rethe (21:11), nec ullus piscium eiectus, quia tunc pax summa erit
in sanctis, et nullum scisma, ubi fuerunt capti pisces .c.l.iii
(i.e. 153), quo significantur omnes ad graciam spiritus sancti per-
80 tinentes, sicut dicitur in glossa. Et hii omnes pisces fuerunt
magni, quia secundum glossam, *in illo dei regno nulli erunt nisi*
magni et spiritales amici, sicut fit et in nupciis carnalibus in
quibus nonnisi spiritales retinentur ad cenandum.
      (7) Item uere magna erit hec cena, et propter ferculorum appo-
85 nendorum in eam multitudinem et preciositatem. Unde cor. (1 Co
2:9), dicitur *quod oculus non uidit nec auris audiuit, nec in cor*
hominis ascendit que preparauit deus diligentibus eum. Et est sensus
ad litteram, quod nullus sensus humanus, nullusque intellectus
potest comprehendere tot uel tanta bona: quot et quanta dabit deus
90 saluandis in eterna beatitudine. Unde Augustinus in libro de ciuitate
dei ultimo. *Quanta erit illa felicitas ubi nullum erit malum,*
nullum latebit bonum, quod dicit, aperte et manifeste erunt ibi
omnia bona celestia terrestria. Idem in eodem, *Deus erit finis*
desideriorum nostrorum qui sine fine uidebitur, sine fastidio ama-
95 *bitur, sine fatigatione laudabitur.*
      (8) Erit eciam hec magna duracione, quia finem non habebit,
quia eterna erit. Unde Mt .25. (25:46), *ibunt uero iusti in uitam*
eternam. Unde Augustinus de ciuitate dei, libro ultimo, de illo
statu sanctorum ubi *uacabimus et uidebimus, et amabimus et laudabi-*
100 *mus. Ecce quod erit in fine sine fine. Nam quis est alius finis*
noster nisi peruenire ad regnum cuius nullus est finis.

---

70. *in inter.* non inueni. 80. Jo 21:11, *non est scissum rethe*; cf. Lc 5:6. 79–83
Glossa . . . glossa, non inueni. 90–92. Aug., *De Ciuitate Dei.,* XXI, c. xxx, lineis 1–2.
93–95. *Idem, in eodem,* lineis 33–35. 98–101. *Idem,* lineis 145–48.

takes place, not only will the joy of the good be greater, but the torment of the wicked will be more oppressive, since they will be tortured in the body according to Matthew 25 (25:34): 'then he will say to those on his right hand,' etc., according to the interlinear, 'only those reaching happiness.'

(6) At this supper along with all mankind destined to be saved will also be the inexpressible armies of the nine choirs of angels, because then all the saints will be like angels as we read in Matthew 22 (22:30). Great also will be the guests at this supper, because there no one can be small as is indicated in the great catch of fish in John 21, when the net was rent (Jn 21:11), 'the net was not rent,' see Lk 5:6), and none of the fish discarded, because then among the saints will exist prefect peace and no schism, when the 153 fish have been caught, by which is meant, as we read in the gloss, all who attain the grace of the holy Spirit. All the fish were great, because according to the gloss: 'in that kingdom of God there will be none but great friends in the Spirit, for this also happens in weddings of the flesh, in which only friends in the spirit are kept for supper.

(7) Likewise this supper will be really great both for the number and the delicacy of the courses to be served for the supper. Hence we read in 1 Corinthians (2:9): 'what no eye ever saw, what no ear heard, what never entered the heart of man, that God has prepared for those who love him.' The literal meaning is that no human sense, no human intellect can grasp so many and such great blessings as God will grant to those who are saved in eternal happiness. Hence Augustine writes in his final book on the City of God: 'how great will be that bliss, when no evil will exist, and no blessing be withheld!' This means that all heavenly and earthly blessings will be openly and obviously present. In the same chapter Augustine says: 'God will be the end of our desires, for he will be seen without end, loved without distraction and praised without weariness.'

(8) This supper will endure in a great succession, because it will have no end, because it will exist forever. Hence we read in Matthew 25 (25:46), 'but the just will go into life everlasting.' Hence in the last book of the City of God, Augustine writes of the final fortune of the saints: 'where we shall rest and gaze and love and praise. Behold what will exist in the end without end. For what end is proper for us but to reach the kingdom which has no end' (*idem* lines 33–35).

(9) Sequitur. *Et uocauit multos* etc. (Lc 14:16), scilicet,
omnes homines, *qui uult omnes saluos fieri* .1. Thi. altero (ms *ultimo;*
1 Tim 2:4). Uult dico non uoluntate beneplaciti, quasi hoc
105 uellet non posse fieri sed uoluntate consilii precepti et permissionis,
quia omnibus omnia dat precepta uite et consilia, permittit
quoque omnes qui uoluerunt ad salutem uenire, et uolentes adiuuat.
Non enim *in omnem terram exiuit sonus* (Ps 18:5) predicacionis apostolorum ad fidem uocantium, immo sine dubio: sic eciam dicitur in
110 Mt. 20. H Mt .21. (20:16, 22:14). *Multi sunt uocati* etc., interlinearis, *ad fidem, pauci uero electi,* interlinearis, *ad regnum.*

(10) Hodie quidem deus multipliciter uocat, scilicet, per
uerba, et per beneficia, per flagella, per internam inspiracionem,
sicut manifestius dictum est in sermone de euangelio dominice in
115 septuagesima (Mt 20:1–16). Et hic dicit Beda in glossa, super illud,
misit hora cene seruum suum dicere inuitatis ut uenirent etc.
(Lc 14:17) *hora cene* (f. 83r) *finis mundi.* Nos enim sumus [ms. sic,

117 [f.82v, ima pagina] ydolum: ita imago ut sit deus . . . (illegibile);
ydolatria: idolorum . . . (illegibile); ydolator . . . (illegibile).

at Paulus: *Non enim scimus*] in quos fines *seculorum deuenerunt,* cor
.x. (1 Co 10:11). *Mittitur seruus quasi ordo predicatorum ad inui-*
120 *tatos per legem et prophetas ut repulso fastidio ad gustandam cenam*
se preparent, quasi iam parata sunt omnia. Chirsto enim immolato:
introitus regni patet.

(11) Illud quoque considerandum est in hoc loco, quod legitur
triplex sancta inuitacio ad hanc cenam. In prima quidem sicut dici-
125 tur in littera omnes se excusauerunt et uenire noluerunt. In secunda multi introducti sunt, sed non impletus fuit locus conuiuii. In
tercia, introducti sunt multi non solum inuitando sed eciam compel-
lendo et sic impletus est numerus preordinatorum ad uitam ut dictum
est.

(12) Igitur primi inuitati se omnes excusauerunt. Unde Beda:
130 *excusat se omnis qui plus terrena quam celestia diligit, eciam si*
ad celestia tendere se dicat. Prima itaque excusacio est per uillam
emptam. Secunda: per empcionem .v. iugorum boum. Tercia: per uxorem

---

110–11. *in inter.* quod non inueni. 114. *in sermone,* Greg. PL 76:1272B. 115–17. *Beda*
92:514B, *Glossa,* 114: 308C. 119–22. Greg. 76:1267A, Beda, 92:514B, Glossa, 114:308C.
123. *Glossa,* 114:308C, Beda, 92:514B. 130–1. *Beda,* 92:514D, Glossa, 114: 308D. 133–5.
Aug. 39:644A, Glossa, 114:308D.

(9) Now what follows? 'And he invited many,' etc. (Lk 14:16), which means everyone according to the second chapter of 1 Timothy (2:4): 'because he wills all people to be saved.' He wills, let me reaffirm, not with the will of his good pleasure, as if he wished this not to happen, but with the will of his counsel, his command and his permission, because to everyone he gives all the precepts and counsels of life. He also permits all who so wish to come to be saved, and he helps those who so wish. For not 'throughout all the earth was heard the voice' (Ps 18:5), of the eloquent apostles summoning to faith, undoubtedly not. So also we read in Matthew 20 and 22 (20:16, 22:14), 'many are called,' etc., where the interlinear adds, 'to the faith;' 'but few are chosen,' where the interlinear adds, 'for the kingdom.'

(10) Today God calls in many ways, namely, through words, blessings, scourges, inner inspirations, as is explained more clearly in the gospel for Septuagesima Sunday (Mt 20:1–16). And here on the text: 'at the time for the supper, he sent his servant to tell his guests to come,' etc. (Lk 14:17), Bede comments in the gloss: 'the time for the supper (f. 83r) is the end of the world.' Indeed we are the ones in 1 Corinthians 10 (10:11), 'upon whom the end of the ages has come.' A servant is sent like an order of preachers, to those invited through the law and the prophets, that by overcoming their distaste they should prepare to savor the supper as if all the preparations had been made, because with the immolation of Christ the entrance to the kingdom is wide open.

(11) In this passage we should also consider that we hear of three holy invitations to this supper. After the first invitation we hear that literally all were unwilling to come and excused themselves. After the second invitation, although many were introduced, the banquet hall was not full. After the third invitation, many were introduced, thanks less to the invitation than to compulsion, and thus, as has been said, the number of those preordained to life was completed.

(12) So all the guests first invited excused themselves. Hence Bede comments: 'everyone who loves earthly more than heavenly blessings, excuses himself, even though he claims to aim at heavenly blessings.' The first excuse is the purchase of a villa; the second, the purchase of five yokes of oxen; the third, the taking of a wife. In explaining the purchase

ductam. Dicit ergo Augustinus hoc exponendo: *in uilla empta domi-
nacio notatur et superbia, habere enim uillam et possidere: est*
135 *homines sibi subdere, uicium malum, uicium primum; superbiam suple.*
Primus enim homo dominari uoluit: quia dominum habere noluit. Primus ergo quasi per superbiam excusatur. Secundus obtendit .v. iuga,
sensus corporis, quia nichil intendit inuestigandum nisi quod per
hos ministratur, et ideo inuitantes ad eternorum cenam non sequi-
140 tur, et fit hec inuitacio per concupisceniam oculorum, *amor enim
terrenarum rerum: uiscus est penarum spiritualium,* quibus, scilicet
uolandum esset ad eternam. Tercius uxorem duxit, quia uoluptas carnis multos impedit. Unde in quadam glossa, eciam hic dicitur exponendo quare dominus hanc parabolam introduxit, quasi uere bonus qui
145 manducabit panem in regno dei, sed dediti terrenis uel curiositati
uel uoluptatibus huius mundi non comedent.

    (13) Secundum Ambrosium uero hec tria genera que a magna cena
uidentur excludi sunt gentiles propter immoderanciam affectionum
temporalium, Iudei qui christum respuentes: iugum legis ceruicibus
150 suis imponunt, qui sunt .v. iuga uerborum uel .v^{v}. libri ueteris
legis, et heretici qui *uelud eua femineo affectu temptant rigorem
fidei et lubrica fluiditate prolabantes . . . lenocinia fluidi dogmatis
affectant intemeratam negligentes pulchritudinem ueritatis.* Et
notandum quod primi duo qui dixerunt, *rogo te habe me excusatum,*
155 secundum Bedam, *humilitatem sonant in uoce dum contempnunt: superbiam habent in accione.* Tercius uero qui uxorem duxit: non peciit
se haberi excusatum, uel quia in coniugio non est manifesta iniquitas, uel quia carnalis uoluptas ita absorbet multos, ut fiant quasi
tota caro, nec aliud cogitant: nisi carnis delicias. Unde Ambro-
160 sius *coniugium non reprehenditur, sed integritas ad maiorem honorem
uocatur.* Et Beda *propter carnis uoluptatem ad cenam domini uenire
fastidiosus recusat.*

    (14) In secunda autem uocacione siue inuitacione introducti
sunt pauperes, interlineari, qui scilicet suo iudicio *infirmi sunt.*

141–42. Aug. 38:646C, Glossa, 114:308D. 143. *Glossa,* 92:515C. 147–53. *Ambrosius*
15:1842BC. 155–6. *Beda,* 92:515C, Glossa, 114:309A. 160–2. *Ambr.* 15:1842A.
162–3. *Beda,* 92:515C, Glossa, 114:309A. 164. *infirmi sunt, Ambr.* 15:515D.

of a villa Augustine comments: 'lordship and pride are underscored, because to have and possess a villa is to subject men to oneself, an evil vice, the first vice.' He means pride. Indeed the first man wanted to be the lord, because he did not want to have a lord. The first guest, then excused himself, it seems, through pride. The second guest alleges as an excuse his five yokes, the bodily senses, because he intends to investigate nothing but what is served by the senses. Therefore he does not follow those who invite him to the supper of the immortals and his invitation becomes (void) through concupiscence of the eyes, because love of earthly possessions is unaware of the spiritual wings, on which of course, one must fly to the eternal supper. The third guest married a wife, for carnal pleasure is a hindrance to many. Hence it is said even here, in a gloss to explain why the Lord introduced this parable: one destined to eat bread in God's kingdom, as it were, is really good; but those addicted to earthly possessions or to idle curiosity or to the pleasures of this world, shall not share that bread.

(13) According to Ambrose, the three classes which seem to be barred from the great supper, are the Gentiles through their excessive affection for temporal possessions, and the Jews who by rejecting Christ impose on their own necks the yoke of the law, that is, the five yokes of the words or the five books of the old law, and the heretics, who 'like Eve with feminine affection attack the firmness of the faith, and stumbling in the slippery flood . . . embrace the enticements of unstable dogma by neglecting the chaste beauty of truth.' Notice that the first two guests, who pleaded: 'I pray for you, hold me excused,' according to Bede, speak with feigned humility, though they are contemptuous; they manifest pride in action. A third, however, who married a wife, does not ask to be excused, either because there is no obvious iniquity in wedlock, or because carnal pleasure so absorbs most, that they become, so to speak, all flesh, and think of nothing but the delights of the flesh. Hence Ambrose comments: 'wedlock is not condemned, but innocence is invited to greater honor.' Bede adds: 'thanks to the pleasures of the flesh, the disdainful refuse to come to the Lord's supper'.

(14) Now in the second call or invitation the poor are introduced, that is, according to the interlinear, 'those who in their own opinion are

165   Unde Ambrosius in glossa. *Cicius ad dominum conuertitur: qui non*
     habet in mundo unde delectetur. Et Gregorius. *Qui multiplicandis*
     diuiciis incumbit: eterni premii non querit. Et debiles, ceci, et
     claudi introducti sunt, id est, qui se humiles dei senciunt reputantes
     fortitudinem spirituali lumine ingenii et gressibus bonorum
170   operum se carere. Unde Beda in glossa. *Notandum quod sicut peccato-*
     res fuerunt qui uenire noluerunt: ita peccatores sunt qui ueniunt.
     Sed superbi peccatores respuuntur, humiles eliguntur. In tercia dei
     (f. 83v) uero inuitacione, sicut dicit Beda in glossa, non dicitur

---

     [f. 83r, ima pagina: quaedam illegibilia] d. . . . . quo omnes quos
     aliquid ea intencione de aliquo dicit. Unde . . . . minus
     amari . . . . posset. Augustinus super Io. fiant . . . .?
     non natus nuper de fine?

     'inuita' sed 'compelle' intrare. Qui enim huius mundi aduersitati-
175   bus fracti ad dei amorem redeunt et a presentis uite desideriis
     corriguntur, quid nisi compulsi ueniunt? Et Gregorius. *Aduersitates*
     que nos hic premunt, ad deum nos ire compellunt.
     (15) Et notandum quod hec inuitacio uel compulsio ad uocatos
     de gentibus uidetur pertinere, per glossam, in qua dicitur in per-
180   sona uocantis serui ad dominum super illud *factum est ut imperasti*
     (Lc 14:22), *multos tales colligimus ex iudeis ad cenam tuam, sed*
     isti locum conuiuii tui non implent. Superest locus ubi gencium
     numerositas suscipiatur. Et in ista ultima uocacione impleta est
     domus domini, scilicet, numero predestinatorum fidelium, quia nume-
185   rus eximpletus non remanebit, ut dicitur in interlineari. Nos itaque
     qui nos peccatores recogniscimus: deum deuote exoremus, ut det
     nobis ita efficaciter uocacionibus suis (sic) obedire: ut cum ceteris
     fidelibus ad cenam eterne beatitudinis mereamur peruenire, in
     qua ipse cenet nobiscum et nos cum eo. Quod nobis prestare digne-
190   tur, etc.

166-7. *Greg.* 76:1279C. 166-7. *Ambr.* 15:1843B, *Beda,* 92:516A. 170-2. *Beda,*
92:515D, *Ambr.* 15:515D, *Greg.* 76:1269C. 173. *Beda* 92:516C, *Glossa* 114:309B.
176-7. *Greg.* 76:1272AB. 179. *per glossam* ex Beda 92:516AB. 181-3. *Glossa* 114:309B,
Beda 92:516A, *Greg.* 76:1270C.

weak.' Hence Ambrose comments in the gloss: 'one who has no source of delight in the world, is more quickly converted to the Lord.' Gregory adds that 'one who takes pains to multiply his wealth, does not seek the wealth of an eternal reward.' The weak, the blind and the lame are introduced, that is, those who in the Lord consider themselves humble, because they weigh strength by the spiritual light of genius and consider that they are low on the ladder of good works. Hence Bede writes in the gloss: 'notice that just as those who refused to come were sinners, so those who came were sinners. While haughty sinners are rebuffed, humble sinners are welcomed.' Yet as Bede says in the gloss: 'in God's third invitation (f. 83v), he does not day "invite!" but "compel!" them to enter.' People broken by the misfortunes of this world, return indeed to the love of God and are cured of their yearnings for the present life. Do they arrive through anything less than compulsion? Gregory also remarks that 'the misfortunes which oppress us here, compel us to go to God.'

(15) Notice that this invitation or constraint seems to apply to those called among the Gentiles, according to the gloss. The report of the summoning servant to his lord: 'as you commanded, Sir, so was it done' (Lk 14:22), the gloss expands as follows: 'many such guests we gathered for your supper from among the Jews, but they do not fill your banquet hall. Space remains to accomodate the great numbers of the Gentiles.' But with that final summons, the Lord's house was filled with the number of predestined believers, because according to the interlinear, the number will not remain incomplete. So we, who recognize ourselves as sinners, devoutly implore God to help us to obey his invitations so effectively, that with other believers we may deserve to reach the supper of eternal happiness, in which he entertains with us and we with him. May the Lord grant our request, amen.

VII. SERLO OF WILTON: AN EXPLANATION OF
THE LORD'S PRAYER[13]

The Lord's Prayer

Introduction: God the Father is our Protector sometimes in Person, sometimes through his Son, at times through the holy Spirit.

Prologue: includes and concludes with three words, Our, heavenly, Father.

Seven petitions: for seven gifts:

1) *wisdom* to know that God is, what God is not, what God is;
2) *understanding* of the power, the wisdom and the joy of the
   kingdom;
3) *counsel* to discern God's will as good, pleasing and perfect;
4) *strength* through the bread that came down from heaven,
   in three loaves, the God-MAN, the GOD-man, the
   GOD-GOD;
5) *knowledge* of the triple debt to God and the triple debt to
   man;
6) *piety* not to be overwhelmed by the flood, the deep, or
   the pit;
7) *fear* of three evils, sin, the devil, hell; the threefold mercy;

Epilogue: petitions are directed to the Father, enlightened by the Son,
and enkindled by the holy Spirit.

[Adscriptio:] Servis christi conseruus eorum serlo dominicam orationem. [Textus] *Protector noster aspice deus et respice in faciem christi tui.*
(Ps 83:10). [Incipit] Protector noster deus pater est, qui suos protegit
5   interdum per se ipsum, interdum per filium, nonnumquam per spiritum
sanctum. Per se ipsum quidem cum potestatiue temperat incursum
potestatis aduerse, ut in iob (2:6) dicens ad sathan, *animam eius serua.*
Similiter et cum liquefaceret ungulas equorum sisare ante faciem debbore,
qualia continentur in libro bellorum domini (Jud 5:1–32), qui liber vir-
10   tutes eius et mirabilia eius que fecit in aduersarios populi sui diligenter ex-
primebat. Per filium autem nos protegit ut est ibi: *scuto circumdabit te ueritas
eius* (Ps 90:5). Ueritas fidei quam filius edocuit contra ignita iacula
inimici, quasi scuto nos munit (Eph 6:16). Inde sancti *per fidem uicerunt*
regna, etc. (Heb 11:33). Per spiritum sanctum uero nos protegit, cum in
15   cordibus nostris ignem sue *dilectionis que fortis est ut mors* infundit (Cant
8:6). Unde dicitur: *scuto bone uoluntatis tue coronasti nos* (Ps
5:13). Hoc scutum spiritus sancti discipuli diuinitus acceperunt *nimisque
confortatus est* sub eo *principatus eorum* (Ps 138:17).
Dicitur ergo: *Protector noster aspice deus pater et respice in faciem*
20   *christi tui* (Ps 83:10). Aspice et respice. Aspice ante te et respice post
te. Aspice in faciem christi filii tui, in gloria presentem et gloriose
splendentem, qualis est ibi nunc post ascensionem et respice in faciem
eiusdem clamantem post te quasi miseram et miserabilem in hac nostra
miseria, qualis fuit hic ante resurrectionem. Aspice in faciem christi tui,
25   qualis est nunc in ipso glorificata et respice in faciem christi tui,
qualis fuit in ipso tunc corruptibilis et quasi leprosa, et est in suis
nunc qui student *sicut ille ambulauit et ipsi ambulare* (Is 53:4, 1 Jo
2:6), hic modo *compatientes* (1 Pet 3:8), ut ibi postmodum conregnent
(2 Tim 2:12). Illic habemus apud patrem aduocatum filium, qui *ascendit in*

Marginalia varia ex mss ON, OR, OT, et S: 1 ad Rom xii, *orationi instantes* (Rm 12:12): ad
Rom viii c (Rm 8:17), *si filii et heredes: heredes quidem dei, coheredes* etc.; item in eodem (loco)
ipse spiritus postulat pro nobis gemitibus inenarabilibus (Rm 8:26): summa pagina, ON.

---

6 *potestatiue*: per potestatem OR; potestate P1; *incursum*: cursum OR, P3. 10 *mirabilia*:
miracula: a, E, G, ON, P5. *aduersarios*: aduersa P3; *sui*: Israel add E. 16 *nos*: eos Au, P6. 19
Dicitur: dicatur P3. 21 *in gloria*: et gloria, P6, in gloriam P3. 23 *miseram*:miserum B. 24
ipso:christo a. 28 *conregnent*: regnent E; *apud*: ad B.

VII. SERLO OF WILTON: AN EXPLANATION OF
THE LORD'S PRAYER

(God our Protector)

[Ascription:] FOR THE SERVANTS OF CHRIST, THEIR FELLOW-SERVANT, SERLO
EXPLAINS THE LORD'S PRAYER. 'O God our Protector, look and see the face
of your anointed' (Ps 83:10). God our Protector is a Father who protects
his children, *sometimes in Person, sometimes through his Son, at times
through his holy Spirit.* Yes, in Person, when through his power he checks
the attack of a hostile power, as he cautioned Satan about Job (2:6), 'but
spare his life.' Similarly, in the sight of Debbora, he melted the hoofs of
the steeds of Sisar, according to the record in the book of the Lord's bat-
tles (Jg 5:1–32), a book which carefully recounts his powers and the
wonders he worked against the foes of his people. As the psalm promises
(90:5), he also protects us through his Son: 'with a shield his truth en-
folds you.' The truth of faith which his Son taught, arms us with a shield
'against the flaming arrows of the foe' (Eph 6:16). Hence the saints
'through faith conquered kingdoms,' etc. (Heb 11:33). Through his holy
Spirit, however, he protects us when he pours into our hearts the fire of
his 'love which is as strong as death' (Sg 8:6). Hence the psalmist says
(5:13): 'you covered them, O God, with the shield of your good will.'
The disciples received from God this shield of the holy Spirit and under
it 'their leadership was exceedingly strengthened' (Ps 138:17).

'Our Protector,' God our Father, says the psalmist (83:10), 'look and
see the face of your anointed.' 'Look and see.' Look before you and after.
Look upon the face of Christ your Son present in glory and resplendent
in glory, as it is in heaven now after his ascension. Look back upon the
face of the same Son, crying after you, pitiable and pitiful, as it were, in
our plight, as his face was here before his resurrection. Look upon the
face of your anointed as it is now glorified in him, and look back on the
face of your anointed, as it was in him on earth, corruptible as if belong-
ing to a leper (Is 53:4) and as it is now in his members, who 'struggle to
walk as he walked' (1 Jn 2:6). They are compassionate here now (1 P
3:8), that hereafter they may reign with him (2 Tm 2:12). As advocate
with the Father in heaven we have his Son, 'who ascended the mountain

30 *montem solus orare* (Mt 14:23), *montem excelsum ualde* (Mt 4:8), scilicet
equalitatem paterne glorie. Ille orat in monte in facie gloriosa, qualem
suis tandem promisit; nos oramus in ualle in facie erumpnosa, cuius exemplum nobis ipse premisit. Orare in ualle nos oportet secundum illud:
subditus esto domino et ora eum (Ps 36:7), quod est: humiliter adora et
35 sic fiducialiter ora. Cum enim fideliter humilitas adorat, necessitas
efficaciter orat et impetrat. Orat itaque christus in monte sancto suo et
exauditur *pro sua reuerentia* (Heb 5:7); nos autem orantes in hac ualle
plorationis exaudiemur pro nostra obedientia (Heb 5:8). Quia uero *sicut
oportet* orare nesciebamus (Rom 8:26), docuit unicus uniuersos, docuit
40 filius naturalis adoptiuos *semper orare et non deficere dicens* (Luc 18:1),
sic orantes dicetis: *Pater noster qui es in celis* (Mt 6:9).

[PROLOGUS]

Pater noster qui es in celis (Mt 6:9). Hec est ergo dominica oratio
ceteris omnibus orationibus et instituentis auctoritate sublimior et uti-
45 litate peticionum fecundior et sapientie doctrina subtilior. Hec oratio
uerbum est abbreuiatum (Is 10:22, Rom 9:28), quod celi dominus fecit in
terra omnia complectens utrobique nobis necessaria. Et quia sapientia

---

35 *ora*: adora OR, P3; *fideliter*: fiducialiter G. 37 ad heb V, b, (5:7) *qui in diebus carnis
sue preces postulationesque (ad) eum qui posset saluum illum facere cum clamore ualido et
lacrimis offerens exauditus est pro sua reuerentia*, marg. *ON*. 37 *adorat*: orat *E*. *pro sua
reuerentia*: propter suam reuerentam d. 38 *orantes*: oramus AD; *exaudiemur*: exaudimur
G, OR. 40 *non*: nunquam E, R. 43 A. S. marg. OT, epositio tribuitur Abbati Serloni;
de dominica oratione habetur Mt vi, Luc xi: ima pagina ON. 47 utrobique: corpori et
anime marg. ON.

---

43 Hic incipit BE. *celis*: Quinque sunt septene. septem uicia (bis). septem uirtutes. vii
peticiones. septem dona. septem beatitudines. Est homo egestus deus medicus. uicia
langores uirtutes ualitudines. peticiones planctus et postulationes. dona antidota.
beatitudines felicitatis gaudia. In oratione itaque dominica sunt septum peticiones, ut
septem donis spiritus sancti mereamur, quibus recipiamus septem uirtutes per quas a
septem uiciis liberati peruenire possimus ad septem beatitudines (5 lineae interpolantur in
P3; cf. Hugonis de S. Victore opusculm, De Quinque Septenis seu septenariis, P L
176:405–414; et Bloomfield, Incipits, nos. 4833, 4835). 45 *fecundior*: facundior BE; *subtilior*: salubrior R.

alone to pray' (Mt 14:23), 'the mountain exceeding high' (Mt 4:8), the mountain of equality with his Father's glory. On the mountain he prays with features glorious, such as he promised to his son at last; in the valley we pray with features emerging in the light of the example he set before us. In the valley it becomes us to pray according to the psalm (36:7): 'be subject to the Lord and pray to him,' that is, adore with humility and so entreat with confidence. For when humility entreats with faith, necessity prays effectively and is heard. Consequently, on his holy mountain Christ prays and is heeded 'for his reverence' (Heb 5:7). Yet praying in this valley of tears, we will be listened to for our obedience (Heb 5:8). But since we did not know how to pray as we ought (Rm 8:26, his only Son by nature taught us all, his children by adoption, 'to pray always and not to lose heart' (Lk 18:1), saying, 'our Father who art in heaven' (Mt 6:9).

(II. THE PROLOGUE)

'Our Father who art in heaven' (Mt 6:9). This is the Lord's prayer. Thanks to the authority of its author, it is more sublime than all other prayers, more valuable in its practical petitions and more subtle in its teaching of wisdom. This prayer is a summary (Is 10:22, Rm 9:28), which the Lord of heaven made on earth to include all our needs on earth and in heaven. Because wisdom delights in a threefold description,

triplici gaudet descriptione, necessarium duximus expositione ternaria
peticiones has septem transcurrere. Huic autem doctrine sue permittit
50 dominus prologum breuem quidem et orationi nostre, quia sic est preparatio
eius, pernecessarium. Hic autem tria uerba complectitur et in tribus
consummatur.

Primum uerbum, scilicet *Pater*, cor hominis confortat (Ps 103:15).
Secundum, scilicet *noster*, cor hominis dilatat (Ps 118:32). Tertium,
55 scilicet *qui es in celis*, cor hominis eleuat et inaltat (Pr 18:12). Pater
se ipsum negare non potest (2 Tim 2:13). Sicut enim uerum est: si mater
est et diligit, sic uerum est, immo uerius: si pater est et diligit. Et
hic pater. Uerius est, inquam, sicut asserit ipse: *si mater obliuiscitur
filium uteri sui, ego tamen non obliuiscar populi mei* (Is 49:15). Ad hunc
60 igitur patrem fiducialiter accedes, etiam si de longinqua regione, etiam
si male consumpta substantia, etiam si tanto patre prorsus indignus redieris (Luc 15:13–20). Cum additur *noster*, ad effusionem fraterne dilectionis erga omnes homines prouocamur. Si enim diceretur *pater mi*, forte
quis insolesceret ceterosque tamquam degeneres pre sua nobilitate quasi
65 singulari contempneret. *Qui es in celis* dicitur, ubi plenius cum suis

---

49 *premittit:* premisit g. 53 *confortat:* confirmat R. 55 *inaltat:* exaltat a, BE, S; Atque sicut
mater consolatur filium suum ita et ego consolor uos, add OT; *potest:* qui suos sic confortat, add OT. 57–8 *Et . . . inquam:* om B. 60 *accedes:* accede, G; accendens M; ac-
cedamus, OT. 62 indignus redieris: indigni redierimus, OT. 62 *fraterne dilectionis:*
dulcedinis superne gratia BE. 64 pre: pro, BE, G. 67 *sed:* longe, add BE; *mirabiliorem:*
contemplatur et, add BE; contemplatur uel, add P3. 68 *uero:* auctoritas, add a.

---

50 prologum: prologus marg. ON. 53 *Pater:* creatione, adoptione, temporalium colla-
tione: summa pagina S. 54 captat paternum affectum per gratiam specialem, uel in secreto
maiestatis sue, uel inuisibilis, summa pagina S. *cor hominis:* non unius populi uel hominis
tantum sed communis, summa pagina S. 64 Bernardus. Nota securum accessum habet
homo ad deum qui cause sue mediatorem habet filium ante patrem, matrem ante filium.
Mater ostendit filio pectus et ubera. Filius patri latus et uulnera. Nec ullo modo poterit
esse repulsus, ubi tot caritatis concurrunt insignia. Mt xvii c, (i.e. post annum 1240). Si
habueritis fidem sicut granum sinapis, dicetis monti huic: transi hinc et nichil impossibile
erit uobis. Mt xix (19:26) omnia possibilia sunt credenti. De operibus trinitatis: in tercio
folio subsequente capitulo. Ecce sic dominus etc., ima pagina ON.

we felt obliged to run through the seven petitions with a triple explanation. Now our Lord begins his teaching with a prologue, brief indeed but
more than necessary for our prayer, since in fact his prologue is a
preparatory prayer. The prologue includes and concludes with three
words. The foremost word, *'Father,'* comforts the hearts of all mankind
(Ps 103:15). The second word, *'our,'* expands the hearts of all (Ps
118:32). The third word, *'heavenly,'* raises and exalts the hearts of all (Pr
18:12). The father 'cannot be untrue to himself' (2 Tm 2:13). Just as it is
a truism to say that if a mother exists, she also loves, so it is true, or
rather it is truer to say, that if a father exists, he also loves. And here is
the Father. It is truer, I insist, as he himself claims: 'if a mother should
forget the child of her womb, still I will not forget my people' (Is 49:15).
Consequently you will approach this father with trust even from a coun-
try far off, even after wasting his substance, even if you return wholly
unworthy of so great a Father (Lk 15:13-20). When to 'Father' he adds
'our,' we are invited to pour out a brother's or a sister's love on all
mankind. Now were he to say 'my' Father, perhaps someone might put
on airs and despise the rest of us as base-born by comparison with a
special child of the blood.

Our Lord says: 'who art in heaven,' because he is more fully glorified gloriatur et ubi facie ad faciem, id est, presens presentem, creatura creatorem, mirabilis quidem sed mirabiliorem speculatur (1 Cor 13:12). Quod si diceretur *qui es ubique*, non dissonaret a uero, sed intellectus noster forsitan et affectus patrem quesiturus in uanum diffunderetur, et

70   qui quasi ubique esset, nusquam esset. *In celis* autem esse dicitur, *ut ibi sit cor tuum ubi est thesaurus tuus* (Mt 6:21), ut illic anheles et omni desiderio suspires, ubi est pater tuus, ubi patria tua, ubi et patrimonium tuum. Si ergo patrem sicut oportet honoramus, si uere patrissamus, id est, *imitatores dei sumus sicut filii karissimi* (Eph 5:1), si proximos

75   et amicos in ipso et inimicos propter ipsum tamquam fratres diligimus, si ibi nostra fixa sint corda ubi uera sunt gaudia, quicquid uoluerimus petemus et fiet nobis (Joan 15:17).

(PRIMA PETITIO, DONUM SAPIENCIE)

Est ergo peticio: *sanctificetur nomen tuum* (Mt 6:9). *Sedentibus in tenebris* (Ps 106:10), primo necessaria est lux, et lux illa que

80   *illuminat omnem hominem uenientem in hunc mundum* (Joan 1:9), que est dei noticia, quam nomen ipsius hic exprimit, nomine quippe suo quidlibet innotescit. Cumque deus spiritus sit (Joan 4:24), nomen illius spiritus quo nihil est spiritualius, noticia eiusdem procul dubio est spiritualis, tripliciter quidem distinguenda: quod sit, quid non sit, quid sit. Prima

85   namque noticia dei est quod sit, secundum illud: *accedentem ad deum primum oportet credere quia est* (Heb 11:6). Brutis enim brutior est *insipiens qui*

---

71. *anbeles . . . suspires:* anhelemus . . . suspiremus OT. 72–73 *tuus . . . tua . . . tuum:* noster . . . nostra . . . nostrum OT. 75 *ipso . . . ipsum:* christo . . . christum, AU, BE. 78 sint: sunt, L, P4.

---

67 monet nos ut simus celi, id est, sancti summa pagina S. 78 *Prima petitio. Donum sapientie.* Beatitudo pacis firmetur in nobis, ut finaliter simus tui per adoptionem, summa pagina S. 79 *lux illa,* Iohannes 1 (1:9), marg. ON. 83 *Noticia dei* tripliciter distinguenda, marg. OT. 86 *insipiens:* Ps (13:1), marg. ON. 81 *exprimit:* imprimit, R; *nomine:* Nomine AD, BE, B, C, D, G, ON, OR, P1; *quidlibet:* C, D, ON, OR, P5; cuilibet, P4; cuilibet uel quidlibet, P1; quilibet, BE, B, C, M, P2, P3; quelibet OT. 84 *quidem:* itaque, d. 87–90: *Illorum . . . non esse:* om, add: Illa enim quasi naturaliter ignorant deum esse, cuius tamen beneficio sortiuntur etiam suum esse. Ille uero nequiter in caput suum mentitur affirmans deum non esse, quod si uerum esset insipiens ipse non esset d;

continued

there with his own, and because there the wonderful creatures present with and in the presence of their more wonderful Creator, 'gaze upon him face to face' (1 Co 13:12). But if he were to say: 'Our Father who art everywhere' he would indeed mirror the truth, but perhaps our understanding and our affection, in search of our Father, would be confused and distracted, as if he who is everywhere, were nowhere. but he says, 'in heaven,' that our hearts may be where our treasure is (Mt 6:21), that with every breath and sigh we may yearn to be there, where our Father is and our fatherland and our father's inheritance. If then we honor our Father as we ought, if we mirror our Father, that is, if as 'most beloved children we are imitators of God' (Ep 5:1), if in him we love our relatives and friends as brothers and sisters, and our enemies for his sake, if our hearts are fixed where true joys exist, we will ask whatever we wish and it will be done for us (Jn 15:17).

[III. THE SEVEN PETITIONS]

(The first, for the gift of wisdom)

Now the first petition is: 'hallowed be your name' (Mt 6:9). 'For those who sit in darkness' (Ps 106:10), the first need is for light and for 'that light which enlightens everyone who enters this world' (Jn 1:9). We need that knowledge of God which his name here expresses, because in his name everything comes to light. Since God is Spirit (Jn 4:24), and since his name is the Spirit, than which nothing is more spiritual, knowledge of the same Spirit is undoubtedly spiritual and requires a threefold clarification: that God exists, what God is not, and what God is. The first truth to know about God is *that he exists*, as we read in Hebrews (11:6): 'one approaching God should first believe that he exists.' More ignorant than the brutes is 'the fool who says in his heart: "God does not

dixit in corde suo: non est deus (Ps 13:1, 52:1). Illorum namque non
reprobat insipientiam, iusticia quam probat natura. Ille uero sic offen-
dens *in uno, reus est omnium* (Jac 2:10), dum temere, nequiter et obstinate
90   pronunciat *omnium esse* non esse.
     Secunda noticia dei est: quid non sit, iuxta illud uiri secundum deum
sensati:[14] non parua portio intelligentie est, dum nondum possumus intelligere quid deus sit, si iam plene intelligimus quid non sit. In hunc modum
philosophis et conquisitoribus huius seculi a creatura mundi creator inno-
95   tuit, creatura qualibet attestante palamque profitente, quidnam sit creator inquirenti: *non sum ego deus tuus, mutabilem me fecit, nec factus
nec mutabilis.* Homines enim predicti *cum sic deum cognouissent, non
sicut deum glorificauerunt aut gratias egerunt, sed euanuerunt in cogitationibus suis,* adeoque *stulti facti sunt* (Rom 1:18–23), ut dicerent
100 lapidi: *deus meus es tu,* et ligno: *tu me genuisti* (Jer 2:27). Tercia
tandem noticia dei est: quid sit, scilicet, ut eum cognoscamus sicut et
cogniti sumus (1 Cor 13:12). Et hec est nobis promissa beatitudo iuxta
illud: *hec est uita eterna ut cognoscant te deum uerum et quem misisti
iesum christum* (Joan 17:3). Hoc nomen, id est, hanc dei noticiam nemo
105 nouit nisi qui accipit (Apoc 2:17), uel hic per fidem uel ibi per speciem.
Tanteque uirtutis est et efficacie hoc nomen ut eius inuocatione per fidem
etiam alienam sanctificentur non sancti, ut in baptismo paruuli cum
dicit etiam ancilla etiam quamlibet infidelis: *baptizo te in nomine patris et
filii et spiritus sancti,* id est, in fide et uirtute future dei noticie.
110 Sic eum nosse uiuere est. Infidelitas autem et nunc sine fide per maliciam
cruciat impios *in umbra mortis* (Job 3:5) quasi morte prima, tandem crucia-
tura miseros per iusticiam in morte secunda tunc in tenebris exterioribus

---

104 Johannes xviii (sic, Joan 17:3) marg. ON. 107 *non sancti:* ut sancti, ON; nomen sancti,
L. 108 *etiam quamlibet:* inv P4; *quamlibet:* quelibet corr OR. 109 *sancti:* Amen add R. 110
Indifelitas autem: Infidelitatem, *corr:* Deinde cum fide christianorum, miserorum, interlin. OR.
113 *speculam:* speculum G, ON, P6; *speciei:* spei P1, P4, P6, 117 *uos . . . uos:* nos . . . nos M.
119 *uidelicet:* scilicet E, g.

---

continued...
Illa . . . esse: P3, add Brutorum non reprobat insipientiam . . . *omnium esse* non esse. *92 intelligentie:* intelligendi, ON. 93 *plene:* plane G, ON; *intelligimus:* intelligamus, E, P4. 95 *profitente:* confitente E. 97 Homines . . . deum: om, add: Illi uero cum deum, B. 97 *cognouissent:*
agnovissent P2; cognouerunt, L. 98–99 *cogitationibus:* cordibus E.

exist"' (Ps 13:1, 52:1). Such folly is rejected and not by the justice which nature esteems. The one who so offends 'on one count is in the dock on all counts of the law' (Jm 2:10), as long as he rashly, wickedly and stubbornly proclaims the non-existence of the supreme being.

The second truth to know is *what God is not*. According to a remark of a man wise in God's ways, as long as we can yet understand what God is, it is no negligible bit of wit, if at last we know fully what God is not. Through this way, to the philosophers and searchers of this world, the Creator of the universe became known from his creation, for every creature testifies and openly confesses to anyone inquiring about the nature of its Creator: 'I am not your God. Uncreated and changeless, he made me the changeable.' Although the people just mentioned knew God in this way, they neither honored nor thanked him as God, but in their reflections they strayed in vain' (Rm 1:18–23). 'They became so fatuous' as to say to a stone, "you are my god," and to a stump, "you begot me"' (Jer 2:27).

The third truth is to know at last *what God is*, that we may know him just as we are known (1 Co 13:12). This is the bliss promised us in John: 'This is eternal life, to know you, the true God, and Jesus Christ whom you have sent' (Jn 17:3). This name, that is, this knowledge of God no one has, except 'one who has received it' (Rv 2:17), either on earth through faith or in heaven through the beatific vision. Of such power and efficacy is this name, that by its invocation even through the faith of another those who are not saints are sanctified, as in infant baptism when even a maidservant or any unbeliever says: 'I baptise you in the name of the Father and of the Son and of the holy Spirit,' that is, in the faith and power of an anticipated knowledge of God. To have such knowledge is to live. Even in this lifetime, the unholy who lack faith through their own fault are crucified 'in the shadow of death' (Jb 3:5), as in a first death, only to be crucified by justice after this lifetime in a second death. Thus 'the shadow of death' in their lifetime obscures the mirror of faith and afterwards a second death, 'in eternal darkness' (Mt

(Mt 8:12), contra speculam speciei. Dicitur ergo *sanctificetur nomen tuum*, ut clarificetur pater in filiis, non blasphemetur (1 Tim 6:1) in
115 nobis ut in nequam seruis. *Sanctificetur*, inquam, id est, sanctum sicut est, in nobis ostendatur, iuxta illud filii, *sanctifico me ipsum* propter uos (Joan 17:19), id est sanctum ostendo, ut et uos ita faciatis. Et prima quidem dei noticia scilicet *quod sit* sanctificat et mundat ab insipientia bruta. Secunda uero, uidelicet *quid deus non sit*, sancti-
120 ficat et purgat ab ydolatria stulta. Tercia uero dei noticia, que est *quid sit*, sanctificat et liberat a morte secunda. His ipsis adapta et ordine ipso tria que dicuntur in psalmo de christo: *posuerunt me in lacu inferiori, in tenebrosis, et in umbra mortis* (Ps 87:7). *In lacu inferiori*, dicentes *non est deus* (Ps 13:1, 52:1); *in tenebrosis, ponentes lucem*
125 *tenebras* (Is 5:20), quasi *ueritatem dei in mendacium* (Rom 1:25) ydoli conuertentes, *et in umbra mortis* (Ps 87:7), lucernam fidei infidelitatis nocte extinguere conantes dicendo: *non faciet deus bonum quod bonis pollicetur et non faciet malum quod malis comminatur* (Ps 10:11–13).

[SECUNDA PETICIO, DONUM INTELLECTUS]

Sequitur secunda peticio: *adueniat regnum tuum* (Matth 6:10). Est autem
130 quasi triplex regnum dei: regnum potencie, regnum sapientie, regnum leticie. Huius regni triformis gloria, sanctos omni uirtutum robore confirmando, omni splendore ueritatis illustrando, omni suauitate iocunditatis infundendo, felicitat in celo quasi sursum gloriosos in solio. Nos autem miseri deorsum sedentes uelut in carcere, uelut in sterquilino colloquimur

120 *noticia*: om, add: que est C, g. 121 *His*: hiis, Au, Be, E, G, L, P2, P5, P6, S. 124 *ponentes*: ponentis P3. 126 *infidelitatis*: infidelitatis P3. 127 *dicendo*: dicentes G, P3; 127 *bonum*: bonum uel quid boni iustis pollicetur et non faciet malum quod malum comminatur R; *non*: si BE. 132 *suauitatis iocunditate* P3. 133 *felicitat*: felicitatis BE. 134 *sterquilino*: sterquilinio, OT, P3.

129 *Secunda petitio*. Donum Intellectus: precipuum filiorum desiderium. Compleatur in presenti et futuro. Societas angelorum. Ut gratia et gloria regnent in nobis expulsa macula, ima pagina S. 130 *regnum dei triplex*, marg. OT; regnum potentie, sapientie, leticie, marg. ON.

8:12), will obscure the slightest hope of the beatific vision. Our Lord says: 'hallowed be your name,' that the Father may be glorified in his children and not blasphemed (1 Tm 6:1) among us, as among worthless servants. 'Hallowed' means that in us he may be shown to be the holiness he is, according to his Son's word: 'for your sake I make myself holy' (Jn 17:19), that is, I show myself holy, that you also may do the same.

Now the first truth about God, namely, *that he exists*, sanctifies and cleanses from brutish ignorance. The second, namely, *what God is not*, sanctifies and purges from the folly of idolators. But the third truth about God, which is *what God is*, sanctifies and frees from the second death. To these three truths, adapt in the same order three statements about Christ in the psalm (87:7): 'they set me in the lower pit, in regions of darkness and in the shadow of death.' 'In the lower pit,' for they said, 'there is no God' (Ps 13:1, 52:1). 'In regions of darkness,' 'for they misprepresented darkness as light' (Is 5:20), as if 'exchanging the truth of god for the falsehood of idols' (Rm 1:25). 'And in the shadow of death' (Ps 87:7), for they struggled in the midnight of faithlesness, to extinguish the lamp of faith by exclaiming: 'God will not make good the good he promises the righteous nor the evil with which he threatens the wicked (Ps 10:11–13).

VII. (THE SECOND, FOR THE GIFT OF UNDERSTANDING)

The second petition is as follows: 'may your kingdom come' (Mt 6:10). God's kingdom is threefold: a kingdom of *power*, a kingdom of *wisdom* and a kingdom of *joy*. The glory of this threefold kingdom delights those in heaven, who are enthroned as it were in glory above, by strengthening the saints with all the power of the virtues, by enlightening them with all the splendor of truth and by pouring into them all the joy of happiness. But we poor folk here below, as if imprisoned and sitting on a dunghill,

135   in infirmitate nostra de potestate illa, in cecitate ista de uisione illa,
      in hac infima tristicia de illa summa leticia. Et dum ad illa respirare
      non possumus, anxie suspiramus, intimis anime medullis desiderantes ut
      nostre corruptionis paries, quasi rumphea, deo gratias, adhuc uersatilis,
      non quasi chaos immobiliter obfirmatum (Lc 16:26) *tollatur de medio,* (1
140   Cor 5:2), *uisitetque nos oriens ex alto* (Lc 1:78) mater nostra celestis
      illa ierusalem (Gal 4:26), quam descendentem uidit iohannes ut aquilla
      uolans et altissima penetrans (Apoc 4:7, 21:2). Sic, sic adueniat regnum
      potencie ad nos infirmos ac debiles roborandos. Adueniat regnum sapiencie,
      ad nos cecos ac fatuos illuminados. Adueniat regnum leticie ad nos
145   tristes ac flebiles consolandos. Adueniat inquam, quia nos ad illud uenire
      nequimus. Excipiat nos de mari sagena diuine gratie, nos enim nequaquam
      possumus erumpere de gurgite condicionis nostre.

                    [TERCIA PETICIO, DONUM CONSILII]

          Tercia peticio est: *Fiat uoluntas tua sicut in celo et in terra* (Mt
      6:10), id est, sicut in angelica, sic et in humana natura. Triplex autem
150   uoluntas dei distinguitur ab ipso. Prima cum dicit, *nolo mortem* peccato-
      ris. Quid ergo uis, domine, de peccatore? Uolo *ut conuertatur et uiuat*
      (Ez 33:11). De secunda dicit ipse: *ignem ueni mittere in terram et quid
      uolo nisi ut* ardeat (Lc 12:49) scilicet ut ardentes et ardenter *de
      uirtute in uirtutem* (Ps 83:8), currere faciat, et *in siti* (Ps 61:5).
155   Profectus et affectus deum diligentis, his est. Tercia uoluntas ipsius
      exprimitur, cum dicit: *Pater uolo ut ubi ego sum, illic sit et minister*

---

139 *chaos:* firmiter et add M. *obfirmatum:* firmatum E; ob firmamentum G. 143 *infirmos:*
miseros et imbecillos BE; *roborandos:* reparandos L. 144 *cecos:* stultos B. 145 *flebiles:*
debiles E; *quia nos:* per nos add OT; *ad illud:* illuc BE; *uenire:* peruenire OT; *nequimus:*
non sufficimus P1; nequaquam sufficimus P3; non possumus BE B, P1, P3; nequaquam
possumus D. 150 *ab ipso:* in ipso ON. 153 *ardeat:* accendatur G. 155 *profectus:* perfectus
P1, P3; *deum:* domini ON, OT; *diligentis:* diligentes G.

---

148 *Teritia petitio.* Donum consilii. Per dilectionem in presenti modo uie; in futuro modo
patrie. Preceptum quidem precipue completur in dilectione, summa pagina S. *Fiat:* sit, id
est, uere, marg. S. in angelis, in nobis hominibus, interlin: S. 149 Mt (6:10) marg. ON.
150 *Uoluntas dei triplex,* marg. OT; De triplici uoluntate dei marg. S. 153 Mt (potius Lc
12:49) marg. ON.

in our weakness discuss their power, in our blindness their vision, and in our depth of depression their peak of happiness. As long as we can not be refreshed by their blessings, we sigh anxiously, yearning from the depths of the soul that the wall of corruptible flesh be removed from our midst (1 Co 5:2), as if a sword were flashed in all directions, thank God (Gen 3:24), rather than as if a chasm were fixed immovably (Lk 16:26).

'Breaking in upon us from on high' may the heavenly Jerusalem, our mother (Ga 4:26) 'visit us' (Lk 1:78), as John saw her 'like an eagle in flight plunging to the depths' (Rv 4:7, 21:2). Thus may your kingdom of power come to strengthen us in our weakness and infirmity. Thus may your kingdom of wisdom come to enlighten us in our blindness and folly. May your kingdom of joy come to console us in our sadness and tears. May your kingdom come to us, yes, because we are unable to come to your kingdom. In the net of divine grace may we be rescued form the deep, for in no way can we by our own efforts emerge from the whirlpool of our present plight.

(THE THIRD, FOR THE GIFT OF COUNSEL)

Here is our third petition: 'May your will be done on earth as it is in heaven' (Mt 6:10), that is, as in the angelic nature so also in our human nature. Now God himself makes a threefold distinction about his will. Of his first will, he says: 'I do not will the death' of the sinner. What then do you will, O Lord, with the sinner? I will 'that he mend his ways . . . and live' (Ez 33:11). About his second will, he says himself: 'I came to cast fire upon earth and what do I will but that it be enkindled?' (Lk 12:49). He intends to make the ardent run 'from virtue to virtue' (Ps 83:8), not only ardently but also 'thirsting' for him (Ps 61:5). This is the progress and affection of one who loves the Lord. He expresses his third will when he says: 'Father, I will that where I am, there also my servant

meus (Joan 12:26). Hec autem uoluntas dei trifaria subtilitate tibi pan-
ditur apostolica, scilicet, *uoluntas dei bona, beneplacens et perfecta*
(Rm 12:2). Bona in remissione, beneplacens in promissione, perfecta in
160 exhibicione. Bona, secundum illud: *confitemini domino, quoniam bonus,*
quoniam in seculum misericordia eius (Ps 105:1). Beneplacens, quia diligentibus se regnum pro beneplacito suo promisit (Jm 2:5), quod eisdem tandem *qui potens est* (Ac 20:32), exhibebit. Et secunda quidem et tercia
eius uoluntas impleta est in celis, non prima, quia spiritus ad se conuer-
165 sos, et stantes et ardentes fecit, et in bono tandem solidauit (1 P 5:10).
In aduersis autem, gladius eius inebriatus est in celo (Is 34:5) et omnino
non parcens uersus est omnibus in crudelem (Jb 30:21). Nobis autem de luto
plasmatis (Ps 118:73), quoniam ipse figulus cognoit figmentum nostrum
(Eccli 33:13), mitigauit *omnem iram suam* (Ps 84:4). Coegit enim eum spiri-
170 tus ut effunderet in nos uiscera misericordie sue (Lc 1:78), ut quamlibet
auersi, possimus ad eum conuerti et misericorditer sanari et mirabiliter
saluari. Petimus igitur, ut post remissionem peccatorum uelit et faciat
in nobis, quod uoluit et fecit in sanctis angelis. He tres peticiones
tripliciter explicite, tria que deo debentur implicita continent. Cum
175 dictur: *sanctificetur nomen tuum,* ecce timor. Cum dicitur: *adueniat*
regnum tuum, ecce honor. Cum dicitur: *fiat uoluntas tua,* ecce amor.
In sanctificatione namque timor est, iuxta illud: *timorem eorum ne timue-*
ritis (1 P 3:14), deum autem nostrum sanctificate (1 P 3:15). Sic in

---

165 apostolus in dominica priam post octauam epiphanie (Rm 12:2) marg. OT. 177
apostolus (1 P 3:14–15) marg. ON; Mt iii (Mt 3:12) *paleas comburet igne inextinguibili,* id
est, malos christianos, ima pagina ON. 177 *amor: Fiat uoluntas tua sicut in celo et in terra.*
Hec est radix omnium cogitationum mirabilium nostrarum, add P5. 178 ne: non, P6;
nostrum: uestrum, C, G, L, ON, OR, P4,
P5.

---

157 *trifaria:* De hac trifaria uoluntate dei apostolus ait B. 163 *qui:* quia C; exhibebit: ex-
hibuit AU, OT. 164 *non:* ut P3. 165 *stantes:* constantes B. 166 *aduersis:* auersis a, C, D,
G, OT, P2, P3, R; auersos: L. 167 *omnibus:* eis B, G; *crudelem:* crudele ON; autem de
luto: uero de limo P5; uero B, G; limo E. 168 *cognouit:* cognoscit OR; mitigauit:
temperauit d. 174 *tripliciter explicite:* triplicate ON.

may be' (Jn 12:26).

God's threefold will is unfolded for us by the subtlety of Paul: 'God's will is good, pleasing and perfect' (Rm 12:2): *good* in forgiveness, *pleasing* in promise, *perfect* in execution; good according to the verse: 'confess to the Lord for he is good, because his mercy endures forever' (Ps 105:1), and pleasing because to those who love him he promises his kingdom at his good pleasure (Jm 2:5) which 'he who is mighty' (Ac 20:32) will finally present to his beloved. Both his second and his third will, though not his first, are fulfilled in heaven, because the Spirit has made firm and fervent and finally confirmed in good (1 P 5:10), those who have turned to him. But for those who turn away, his 'sword has drunk its fill in the heavens' (Is 34:5), and utterly unsparing has turned cruel towards them all (Jb 30:21). Yet for us figurines of clay (Ps 118:73), because as the potter he knew our fashioning (Si 33:13), he softened all his anger (Ps 84:4). Indeed the Spirit constrained him to pour into us the marrow of his mercy (Lk 1:78), that we who once turned away might turn back to him and be mercifully healed and wondrously saved. Therefore we ask, that after the remission of sins he should will and perfect in us what he willed and perfected in the holy angels.

The first three petitions explained in this threefold way implicitly contain three debts owed to God. When the Lord says: 'hallowed be your name,' behold the fear of the Lord. When he says: 'your kingdom come,' behold his honor. When he says: 'Your will be done,' behold his love, For in sanctification, there is fear according to Peter: 'have no fear of them. . . . but reverence your God' (1 P 3:14–15). Thus in his kingdom,

regno spendet honor, et in uoluntate feruet amor.

180   Quarta peticio sequitur: *Panem nostrum cotidianum da nobis hodie*
(Mt 6:11). Hec quarta peticio inter tres dictas et tres dicendas media-
stina ponitur, ut in miseria quam exprimunt sequentia, nos reficiat spe et
ad gloriam quam requirunt antecedentia saginando quandoque confortet in
re et sic de hac regione dissimilitudinis et ualle siluestri, quasi de manu
185   iezabel, *in fortitudine cibi illius* perueniamus *ad montem dei oreb* (3
R 19:8). Domine iesu, commoda nobis tres panes in tuo triduo (Lc 11:5),
qui dixisti: *hodie et cras ego operor et tercia die consummor* (Lc 13:32).
Prima dies, hec uita est carnalis, dum vegetatum corpus anima. Secundus
dies uita spiritiualis est, quam sine corpore uiuit anima. Tercius dies
190   erit, *cum tradiderit christus regnum deo et patri* (1 Co 15:24), in corporis simul et anime duplici stola. Domine, da nobis hodie panem qui sufficiat cotidie, panem qui de celo descendit (Jo 6:33), panem te ipsum,
bone iesu, quo nichil gustu suauius, nichil esu salubrius.

Tripliciter enim quasi triplici panetuos pascis te ipso. Et est
195   primus panis, ut sic dicatur, deus homo, panis subcinericius, tuis quidem
solidissimus panis (Heb 5:14), sed hosti *gladius domini et gedeonis*
(Jud 6:20; 7:13). Quid est deus, nisi uita et panis? Et quid est homo,
nisi puluis et cinis? Et quid est in una persona deus latens et homo apparens, nisi panis subcinericius? (3 R 17:13) Quasi deus occultus et homo

---

180 *Quarta peticio* donum fortitudinis, scilicet, ut ad hoc robusti simus, nec in uia deficiamus.
Panem spiritualem, Iusticiam, Sacramenta, Obseruationem preceptorum, Temporalia. *Hodie:*
quamdiu durat hodie, id est, statue presentis milicie. Est panis: Penitencialis: unde *cibabis nos
pane lacrimarum et potum dabis in lacrimis et tunc in mensura* (Ps 79:6); hic est amarus. Doc-
trinalis: unde *non in solo pane uiuit homo, sed in omni uerbo*, et cetera" (Deut 8:3; Mt 4:4; Lc
4:4); hic est dulcis et suauis. Sacramentalis: unde *panis quem ego dabo, caro mea est*, et cetera
(Jo 6:52); hic est supercelestis. Bone operationis: unde *cibus meus est, ut faciatis uoluntatem
patris mei* (Jo 4:34); hic est laboriosus. Eterne beatitudinis: unde *beatus est, qui manducat
panem in regno celorum* (Lc 14:15); hic est infinite dulcedinis, ima pagina S. 186 Dies eius
tres, panis triplex marg. ON. 197 Lucas xiii (13:32) marg. ON.

---

184 *sic:* si S; *siluestri:* si uestri P2. 188 *Secundus:* secunda, Be, B, d, L, OT, P6. 189 *quam,*
qua C, d, G, OR, OT, S; 189 *Tercius:* tercia BE, C, D, G, P1. 191-2 *sufficiat:* sufficit P3.
192 *descendit:* concede, add P6. 193 *bone:* domine, E; *iesu:* quo nichil menti delectabilior, add
BE. 195 *tuis:* tuus BE. 196 *hosti:* hostibus C. 198-9 *apparens:* stans, B.

honor will shine bright and in his will, love will leap like a flame.

(FOR THE GIFT OF STRENGTH)

The fourth petition follows: 'give us today our daily bread' (Mt 6:11). This petition is placed centrally between the three already spoken and the three about to be spoken. Indeed, during the distress which the last three petitions express, this petition may refresh us by anticipation, and by making us fully fit may finally strenthen us in fact for the glory which the first three petitions presuppose. Thus from our region of unlikeness and from our wooded valley, as from the hand of Jezabel, we may arrive 'in the strength of this food at the mountain of the God of Horeb' (1 K 19:8). Lord Jesus, provide us with three loaves for your triduum (Lk 11:5). You said: 'today and tomorrow' I toil, 'and on the third day I reach my goal' (Lk 13:32). The first day is this life in the flesh, as long as the body is quickened by the soul. The second day is the life of the spirit, while the soul lives without the body. The third day will be life in the double robe of body and soul, when Christ 'shall have surrendered the kingdom to God the Father' (1 Co 15:24). Lord, give us today the loaf which is sufficient for each day, 'the bread which comes down from heaven' (Jn 6:33), yourself the Bread, good Jesus, for nothing is sweeter to the taste and nothing healthier for the hungry. Yes, in three ways you feed your own with yourself, as if with bread of three kinds. The first bread we may call the *God-MAN,* a loaf baked under ashes, the firmest bread indeed for your people (Heb 5:14), but for your foe 'the sword of the Lord and of Gideon' (Jg 6:20, 7:13 and 20). What is God, if not life and bread? And what is man, if not dust and ashes? And what is God invisible, and man visible, in one person, if not a loaf baked under ashes, as if God were in hiding and man made manifest? (1 K 17:13). Let this loaf

200   manifestus. Reuersetur hic panis, ut cinis sit in occulto (Os 7:8), et
       cibus in propatulo, eritque panis secundus ut dicatur homo deus. In priore
       panis cinerem portat, in secundo panis cinerem celat, ibi quasi in corrup-
       tionem miserabiliter uadens, hic corruptionem mirabiliter euadens. Hinc
       est quod dominus in humanitate passibili et manifesta, diuinitatem quam in
205   se credi uoluit, mundo predicauit occultam. Post resurrectionem uero de
       diuinitate ipsius nichil hesitantibus et se spiritum uidere estimatibus
       (Lc 24:17) et tactu et esu et in multis argumentis se uerum licet oc-
       cultum probauit hominem.
           Est ergo primus panis subcinericius deus homo, secundus reuersatus
210   homo deus. Subcinericius ante mortem, reuersatus post resurrectionem.
       Sane tercius nec subcinericius, nec supercinericius, superius inferius,
       sine cinere, sine zimate, sine furfure, de simila purissima, non de hac et
       illa natura, omnia reficit nec deficit, semper pulcher et candidus, semper
       recens et calidus, numquam mutandus in sabbato (Lv 24:5–9), nunquam
215   tollendus pro altero. Hic autem quis? Deus deus. Panis quidem super-
       angelicus, supercelestis, supersubstantialis. Deus deus, geminatio rumi-
       nantis est non numerantis. Deuotioni namque non sufficit semel dicere
       deus, nec sine *meus*, quia uox deuota est *deus deus meus* (Ps 21:2).
       Hec faciat mihi deus et hec addat: ut sit *deus, deus, meus*.
220   Quid enim michi proderit deus, si non sit meus? Primus ergo panis,
       cibus est in peregrinatione corporis et anime, ut sequamur uestigia
       christi, *in sanctitate et iusticia omnibus diebus nostris* (Lc 1:75).
       Secundus panis cibus est solius anime in expectatione dicentis: *Domine,*

---

200 *occulto:* manifesto E. 203 *Hinc:* hic, OR, P5. 206 *estimantibus:* existimantibus, P3, R;
estimantibus uel credentibus BE; *spiritum:* ipsum, a BE, B, C, E, ON, OT, S. 211
nec . . . inferius: nec subcinericius est superius, nec subcinericius est inferius, a; sed tam inferius quam superius est, B; sed tam superius quam inferius, G. 212 *simila:* similia, P4;
farinula (3 R 17:13) P6. 121 *non:* Nam, g. 215 *quis:* quid, G. 218 *iterato:* iteratio M, S.
220 *si non:* nisi, BE, B, G, OT. 221 *peregrinatione:* pegerinationis, P2; peregrinationem,
S. 222 *nostris:* uite nostre, E, G. 223 *solius:* solidus, BE.

be reversed, so that the ashes are hidden (Os 7:8), and the food is revealed. Then a second loaf will exist, to be called the *man-GOD*. In the former loaf the bread supports the ashes, in the second loaf the bread conceals the ashes; in the former as if the bread were pathetically passing into corruption, in the latter as if the bread were wonderfully bypassing corruption. The first loaf exists, because the Lord in his suffering and visible humanity preached to the world his hidden divinity, which he wished men to believe present in himself. But after his resurrection, to those who had no hesitation about his divinity and thought 'they saw a ghost' (Lk 24:17), by touching and by eating and by many proofs he showed himself a real but hidden man. Hence the first bread is the loaf baked under ashes, the God-MAN. The second is the loaf reversed, the man-GOD. Before his death he is the loaf baked under ashes; after his resurrection he is the loaf reversed. Certainly the third bread is a loaf baked neither under ashes nor over ashes, but an upside-down loaf, without ashes, without a loaf-pan and without bran, a loaf made of the finest wheat and not a mixture of this nature and of that. This loaf refreshes all things and never fails. This loaf is ever beautiful and bright, ever fresh and warm, never to be changed on the Sabbath (Lv 24:5–9), never to be removed for another. But who is this Loaf? This is the *GOD-GOD*, not the god of an enumerator who counts gods, but of a ruminant savoring the one GOD. Indeed it does not satisfy the devout to invoke God once or twice, unless he adds 'my' God, for the cry of the devout is 'O God, my God' (Ps 21:2). May God perfect this for me and add that he is 'God, my God,' for what will God profit me, unless he be mine?

The first bread, then, is food on our pilgrimage of body and soul, that we may follow the footsteps of Christ, 'in holiness and righteousness all the days of our life' (Lk 1:75). The second bread is the food of that soul only, which says in expectation: 'O Lord, you have singularly founded

singulariter in spe constituisti me (Ps 4:10). Tu enim reformabis *corpus*
225 *humilitatis nostre, configuratum corpori claritatis* tue (Phil 3:21). Tercius panis cibus est delicatorum, in diuinitatis admiratione. Delicatorum
hunc cibum dixerim, qui non fastidientes humanitatem christi, sed trans-
cendentes ad amplius quo nichil amplius, primatum dulcoris in ipsius diui-
nitate feliciter inueniunt, sicut paulus idipsum aliquantisper pregustans
230 dixit: *et si cognouimus christum secundum carnem, sed iam nunc non noui-*
mus (2 Co 5:16).

Quinta peticio est: *et dimitte nobis debita nostra sicut et nos*
dimittimus debitoribus nostris (Mt 6:12). Debita uocantur peccata. Sed
quomodo sunt debita que nulli possunt deberi, nulli debent solui? Cui enim
235 debentur periuria? Cui cetera flagicia? Dicuntur tamen peccata dimitti,
sed methaphorice, quasi debita. Inde namque peccata contraximus, quia
debita non soluimus, id est, non fecimus quod debuimus et ob hoc iudici
penam debemus. Tria igitur ut proprie loquamur debemus deo, totidemque
proximo. Deo reuerentiam, obedientiam, patientiam: reuerentiam maiestati,
240 obedientiam ueritati, patientiam benignitati. Maiestati quidem debemus
reuerentiam, tam terribiliter intonanti et tam horribilia comminanti, que
potest scilicet corpus et animam mittere in gehennam. Ueritati uero debemus obedientiam, tam salubriter instruenti et tam sancta proponenti. Ad
ipsam enim pertinent mandata, sicut scriptum est: *omnia mandata tua*
245 *ueritas* (Ps 118:86). Benignitati etiam debemus patientiam tam iocunde
spiranti et tam felicia pollicitanti, iuxta illud: *momentaneum hoc et*

---

224 Ps (4:10) marg. ON. Apostolus (Ph 3:21) marg. ON. 239 Apostolus (2 Co
5:16) marg. ON. 232 *Quinta peticio:* Donum scientie. Et si quidem culpam incurrimus;
nostra: propter que debitores sumus pene. Da utrumque: et ut dimittas et
nos debito modo dimittamus, summa pagina S. 238 Deo tria debemus; proximo
tria debemus, marg. ON. 245 Ps (118:86) marg. ON. 247 Apostolus (2 Co 4:17) marg.
ON. 258 (32:5) marg. ON. 259 Lucas (6:36) marg. ON.

---

224 *Tu . . . reformabis:* Ipse . . . reformabit, OT. 225 *tue:* sue, ON. 226 *diuinitatis:* contemplatione et, add AD, B. 226–229 *Delicatorum . . . sicut:* om, add, cuius dulcorem paulus
paulisper pregustatus ait OT. 229 *inueniunt:* adueniunt ON. 233 *uocantur:* uocat a, E, G, L,
OT, R; uocant C, L, ON, P2; *peccata:* quia debentur, add AU. 234 *debent:* solent, Au; *solui:*
reddi, B. 235 *peccata:* debita, P6. 236 *contraximus:* trahimus, G; traximus, OT. 237 *quod:*
que, AD, M, P6, 241 *que:* qui, G, P6; quod, a, B. 246 *spiranti:* inspiranti, a, g, ON, S. 246
pollicitanti: pollicenti BE, B, C, E, P5, S.

me in hope' (Ps 4:10). You will indeed reform 'our lowly body to be like your resplendent body' (Ph 3:21). The third bread is the food of the discriminating who marvel at his Godhead. I would call this the food of the discriminating, who without slighting the humanity of Christ, yet reaching an unmatched plateau, happily discover the peak of attraction in the Godhead of Christ, just as Paul after a brief foretaste of Christ's Godhead, exclaimed: 'Even if we once knew Christ in the flesh, that is not how we know him now' (2 Co 5:16).

(FOR THE GIFT OF KNOWLEDGE)

This is the fifth petition: 'and forgive us our debts as we also forgive our debtors' (Mt 6:12). Sins are called debts. But how are sins debts, when they can be owed to nobody, paid to nobody? To whom is perjury owed? To whom are other crimes owed? Sins are said to be forgiven, but metaphorically, as if they were debts. Indeed we have contracted debts by our sins, because we have not paid our debts, that is, we have not done what we ought and therefore we owe a penalty to the judge.

Accordingly, to speak without metaphor, we owe *a triple debt to God* and *a triple debt to our neighbor*. To God, we owe reverence, obedience and patience. We owe reverence to his Majesty with his terrifying thunder and his horrifying threats, which can send body and soul to gehenna. We owe obedience to his Truth, since his instruction is so salutary and his commands so holy, for his commandments pertain to truth according to the Psalm (118:86): 'all your commandments are truth.' We also owe patience to his Kindness, for it inspires so joyously and promises such happiness according to Paul: 'for this light and

leue tribulationis eternum glorie pondus operatur in nobis (2 Cor 4:17).
Hec deo in etate nostra iam effluxa, cuius dampna resarcire non ualet etas
alia, quia quelibet etas quantum preualet, pro se ipsa debet et hec nobis
250 dimitti petimus, scilicet, reuerentiam, obedientiam, patientiam, que deo
tamquam debita non soluimus, et ob hoc rei tenemur. Proximo autem
debemus posse nostrum, nosse nostrum, uelle nostrum. Posse nostrum
proximo debemus in subsidiis, nosse nostrum in consiliis, uelle nostrum in
desideriis. In subsidiis mendico, in consiliis indiscreto, in desideriis peruerso.
255 Dicimus ergo: *dimitte nobis debita nostra sicut et nos dimittimus debitoribus*
nostris. Pater noster deus pacis est. Lites et contentiones a domo sua
procul omnesque rebelliones eliminat, precipiens et admonens, ut *miseri-*
cordia domini plena sit terra nostra (Ps 32:5), filiique misericordie misericordes sint, *sicut et pater eorum celestis misericors est* (Lc 6:36).
260   Sequitur sexta peticio: *et ne nos inducas in temptationem,* id est,
ne nos induci, quod est omnino seduci, permittas. Triplicem quidem temptationem sub hac breuitate psalmus exprimit: *non me demergat tempestas*
aque, etc. (Ps 68:16). Tempestas aque, uiolenta scilicet in aduersis
tribulatio. *Neque absorbeat me profundum,* fraudulenta in prosperis delec-
270 tatio. *Neque urgeat super me puteus os suum,* res periculosissima,
desperatio. *Non me demergat tempestas aque,* temptatio uincens in aduersis,
sed nolentem. *Neque absorbeat me profundum,* temptatio demulcens in prosperis et quasi uiuum degluciens, id est, uolentem. Et est hic profundum
non ibi, quia minus elongat a deo peccans inuitus quam ultroneus (Exod
275 25:2), abstractus quam illectus, id est, nolens quam uolens. Hic autem
absorbetur uoluntas ipsa, unde mors si mala, uita si bona, procedit. Et de

---

260 *Sexta peticio.* Donum pietatis, dimissa iniquitate, ima pagina S; temptatio triplex, marg.
OT. 281 de petro: Mt (16:23); de dauid: ii Regum xi (2 S 11:2 ff.) marg. ON; de ahithophel
(sic): ii Reg xvi (2 S 16:20 ff., de eius morte 17:23); de iuda: Acta Apsotolorum (1:18), marg.
ON.

---

248 *Hec:* hoc, B; *deo:* ideo, G. 249 *alia:* altera, a, OT, P1, P3, P4, S; *pro se ipsa:* per se ipsam
E; *hec:* hoc P6. 250 *que:* quas, AD, C, E, P1, P4, P6. 261 *quod:* id E. 270 *periculosissima:*
periculosa, C, OR. 273 *Et:* Sed, D, (marg.), G, OR. 274 *elongat:* elongatur, BE, L; *ultroneus:*
ultro, BE. 276 *ipsa:* nostra, P6. 277 *urserit:* clauserit, E.

momentary distress . . . is preparing for us a store of eternal glory' (2 Co 4:17). These debts we owe to God in our lifetime now lapsing. Another's lifetime cannot repair the damage, because each lifetime is accountable for a debt in proportion to its own responsibility. Now we ask that these debts be forgiven us, namely, reverence, obedience and patience, debts we failed to pay to God, and for which we are held accountable. To our neighbor, we owe our strength, our knowledge and our determination. To our neighbor, we owe our strength in assistance, our knowledge in counsel, and our determination in acts of good will: assistance to the begger, counsel to the indiscreet and good will to the wicked. Hence we say: 'forgive us our debts' and so forth (Mt 6:12). Our Father is a God of peace. Lawsuits and quarrels and all rebellions he drives far from his threshold. He advises and warns that 'our land' should be 'full of the mercy of the Lord' (Ps 32:5), and that the sons of mercy should be merciful 'as their heavenly Father is merciful' (Lk 6:36).

(FOR THE GIFT OF PIETY)

Here follows the sixth petition: 'and lead us not into temptation' (Mt 6:13), that is, do not permit us to be misled, which means to be entirely seduced. One psalm expresses the triple temptation succinctly indeed: 'let not the flood sweep over me' (Ps 68:16). *The flood,'* means violent tribulation in adversity. 'Nor let the deep engulf me;' *'the deep.'* is the deceitful pleasures of prosperity. 'Let not the pit close its mouth over me;' *'the pit,'* means that most perilous reality, despair, 'Let not the flood sweep over me,' means temptation in adversity, triumphant over one who resists. 'Let not the deep engulf me,' means temptation in prosperity, alluring and swallowing alive one who yields. But the deep is here not hereafter, because one who sins reluctantly rather than voluntarily, drifts less far from God, just as one trapped strays less than another enticed; the unwilling drifts less than the willing. On earth the will is itself engulfed. Hence death, if the will is evil, and life, if the will is good, comes

hoc profundo clamare licet, *si non urserit super nos puteus os suum* (Ps 68:
18). Puteus abyssi, desperatio, que si opilauerit super te os suum, non
te sinet ad penitenciam aperire os tuum, et sic a mortuo quasi qui non sit
280   peribit confessio. Prima autem temptatio petrum abstraxit et impulit ad
negandum; secunda dauid illexit et incendit ad mechandum; tercia achitofel
sicut et iudam suffocauit et traxit ad laqueum.

Septima peticio est: *sed libera nos a malo* (Mt 6:13). Aduersatiua
coniunctio non hic aduersatiue ponitur, ut hic aliquid de dictis quasi cor-
285   rigendo subtrahendum conicias, sed subiunctiue potius ut iam positis, quod
supponitur adicias, quasi dicat: non tantum hec nobis facias, sed etiam
quod sequitur peticionibus nostris accumules, scilicet, ut a malo nos libe-
res, a malo triplici: a malo quod inquinat, a malo quod inquietat, a malo
quod deuorat; a malo quod inquinat, id est a peccato: a malo quod inquie-
290   tat, id est a diabolo: a malo quod deuorat, id est ab inferno. Contra
hanc triplicem miseriam: culpe, pugne, pene, triplicem petiit misericordiam
psalmista: contra culpam clamans: *miserere mei deus secundum magnam mise-
recordiam tuam* (Ps 50:13), in hoc psalmo petens absolui misericorditer a
culpa. Clamat itidem et in alio psalmo: *miserere mei deus quoniam con-*
295   *culcauit me homo* (Ps 55:2), liberari cupiens a pugna. Tercio clamat in

---

280 *peribit:* perit, C, E. 283 *Septima peticio:* Donum timoris, ima pagina S. 288 malum triplex,
marg. OT; triplex malum: culpe, pugne, pene: ima pagina ON; ima pagina S, mala sequentia:

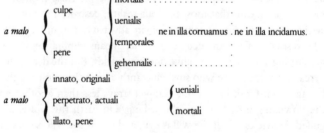

---

281 *illexit:* ille sit E; *incendit:* accendti OR; impulit D, P1. 282 *traxit:* contraxit, R. 284 *dictis:*
positis, d. 291 *petiit:* petit, OR, P3; *clamans:* clamat, Au, E. 294 *alio:* altero, AD, AU, B, E, L,
ON, OR, P5, P6, R, S.

on apace and one may cry from this depth: 'O that the pit might not close its mouth over us' (Ps 68:18). 'The pit,' means the depth of despair, because if the pit closes its mouth over you, it will not allow you to open your mouth in repentance, and so confession will abandon the dead as if he did not exist. The first temptation swept Peter away and prompted his denial. The second allured David and fanned the flame of adultery. The third choked Achitophel no less than Judas and dragged them into the pit.

(FOR THE GIFT OF FEAR)

7. This is the seventh petition: 'But deliver us from evil' (Mt 6:13). The adversative conjunction is not used here in an adversative sense, nor should we assume that by way of correction something should here be withdrawn from what has been said. Rather we may add the conjunction 'but' subjunctively, as an addition to what has been said, as if one were to say: not only do this for us but also add what follows to our previous petitions: namely, 'deliver us from evil.' Free us from a threefold evil: evil which defiles, evil which disquiets, evil which engulfs. *Evil which defiles is sin: evil which disquiets is the devil; evil which engulfs is hell.* Against this threefold misery of our fault, our combat and our chastisement, the psalmist after a fall pleads for a threefold mercy: 'have mercy on me, O God, according to your great mercy' (Ps 50:13); here he begs to be mercifully absolved from his fault. He cried likewise in another psalm (55:2): 'have mercy on me, O God, for all day long the foeman oppresses me;' he yearns to be freed from the strife. He cries out a third time in the psalm

psalmo: *miserere mei, deus, miserere mei* (Ps 56:2), in corpore simul et anima saluari desiderans et eripi prorsus a pena. Hoc autem desiderium pauperum exaudiet dominus, cum impleuerit in fine, quod habet hic psalmus in fine (56:12), scilicet: *Exaltare super celos deus et super omnem ter-*
300 *ram gloria tua* (Ps 56:12).

Ecce sic dominus orare nos docet, ut tripliciter innotescant peticiones nostre apud deum, scilicet, ut ad patrem dirigatur intentio, et intellectus illuminetur a filio, et affectus inflammetur a spiritu sancto, sicque iam spiritalis non animalis animus, et intelligens et diligens, desi-
305 derium iaculetur in altissima, in odorem suauissimum domino. Nec displicebit beate trinitati in manu fidelis abrahe, hostia triplex et trina, cui placuit ut uniuerso semini ipsius in tribus innotesceret unaqueque persona. Pater ut ibi: *numquid non ipse est pater tuus, qui possedit et fecit et creauit te?* (Deut 32:6). Creauit in massa, fecit in persona, posse-
310 dit in iusticia, possessurus in gloria. Filius autem tripliciter innotescit, cum dicit: *Ego sum uia, ueritas et uita* (Joan 14:6) uia que tendit, ueritas que ostendit, uita que comprehendit. In uia, dicit intentio: summum bonum ubi est. In ueritate, dicit cognitio: ecce, hic est. In uita, dicit delectatio: ecce, sic est. Spiritus sanctus quoque in tri-
315 bus declaratur, cum dicitur: *Ille arguet mundum de peccato, et de iusticia et de iudicio* (Joan 16:8). Spiritus rectus, spiritus sanctus, spiritus principalis (Ps 50:14); corrigens (Pr 21:29), dirigens et erigens. Spiritus rectus iniquitatem persequitur, quam mundus amplectitur, et arguit mundum de peccato. Spiritus sanctus equitatem fouet et approbat, quam

---

297 *saluari:* cupiens uel add R. 298 *dominus:* deus, E; *psalmus in fine:* in superficie, P3. 304 *spiritalis:* spiritualis, d. 306 *beate:* beatissime, E; *abrahe:* haberi, P6. 307 *placuit:* complacuit, a, ON, S; ipsius: eius. d, P4. 308 *numquid:* non quid, B. 310 *possessurus:* possidebit, B. 312 *tendit:* ostendit, OR. 313 *hic:* sic, BE. 318 *persequitur:* persequens, BE. 317 amplectitur: complectitur BE.

(56:2): 'have mercy on me, O God, have mercy on me;' he desires to be saved in body and soul alike and to be rescued fully from punishment. Our Lord will grant this desire of the poor, when he comes to the full conclusion with which this psalm ends: 'be exalted above the heavens, O God! Let your glory be over all the earth!' (Ps 56:12).

(IV. *Epilogue*)

See how the Lord teaches us to pray, that our petitions may become known to God in a triple way: that our intention may be *directed to the Father*, our understanding *enlightened by the Son* and our affection *enkindled by the holy Spirit*. Thus also our spirit (*animus*), no longer animal but spiritual, understanding and loving, may project its yearning to the height in an aroma most sweet to the Lord. Nor will a threefold and triple offering in the hand of Abraham the believer be displeasing to the Trinity, for it pleased the Trinity that each person of the three become known to all Abraham's seed. The Father as he is in heaven: 'is he not personally your Father, since he posesses and made and created you?' (Deut 32:6). He created in the mass, he made in person, he possesses in justice, intending to possess in glory. The son makes himself known, however, in a threefold manner, when he says: 'I am the way, the truth and the life' (Jn 14:6). The way guides, the truth teaches, and the life embraces. On the way our purpose tells where the supreme good exists; in the truth our recognition says: look! it is here; in the life, our delight says: look! it is so. The holy Spirit is also proclaimed in a threefold assertion: 'he will convince the world of sin and of righteousness and of judgment' (Jn 16:8). He is the upright Spirit, the holy Spirit, the crowning Spirit (Ps 50:14), correcting (Pr 21:29), directing and uplifting. The upright Spirit prosecutes the wickedness, which the world embraces, and thus 'convicts the world of sin'. The holy Spirit cherishes and approves of

320 mundus odit ac reprobat, et ob hoc arguit mundum de iusticia. De iudicio
uero mundum arguit spiritus principalis, qui principalia et in omnibus
principaliter attendenda, scilicet, iniquitatis et equitatis diuersa stipendia ante oculos timoris et amoris in fine proponit, a quibus mundus
aures auertit. Hec autem sunt stipendia: supplicia deorsum iacentis in-
325 ferni et delicie sursum prominentis paradisi. Ab illis suppliciis suppli-
ces suos nos liberet, et ad illas delicias dilectores suos nos assumat,
summe bonus, immo summum bonum, dulcedo cordium iesus, qui est
benedictus in secula. Amen.

---

321 *principalis:* principia, S. *qui:* quia, E, ON, OR; 324 *aures:* aurem, P6. 326 *bonus:*
summus, E.

328   ⎧ fiat: ⎧ unde et Amen dicitur. Christus quia uerax et semper
           ⎨ fideliter: ⎨ fidelis et quod uult precipit fieri fit;

Amen: ⎧ uerum;   ⎧ unde in apocalypsi (3:14) *Hec dicit Amen*
           ⎨ semper: ⎨ *testis fidelis.*
    Amen confirmatio est, id est, ita fiat et currit confirmando per singulas
peticiones, et est alibi, si fas esset dicere, quasi iuratio domini, qui etsi
non confirmaret mentiri tamen non posset. Et est Amen nec grecum, nec latinum,
sed hebreum, et interpretatur etiam uerum. Sed e contra nec latinus nec grecus
ausus est interpretari, ut diceret uerum. Dico, ne uilesceret mandatum. Et
est nouo testamento quasi iuramentum dei. In uerteri autem: *uiuit dominus* et
cetera, (Deut 27:15 ff.; Jer 4:2, 12:16, Is 65:16). In aliis euangeliis simpliciter dicitur *Amen,* in ioanne geminatur, secundum illud: *sit sermo uester: 'est, est'* (Mt
5:37; Jac 5:12), ut quod ore dicis, operibus comprobes. Ima
pagina S.

(Explicit tractatus de oratione dominica. Incipit libellus: Comparatio clibani
claustri et uirginalis uteri: d. (Ricardi de S. Victore). Vide B. Hauréau,
Notices et extraits de Quelques Manuscripts Latins de la Bibliothèque Nationale,
I:125–126.)

equity, which the world loathes and reproaches, and therefore "convinces the world of righteousness." But the crowning Spirit "convinces the world of judgment, because before the eyes of fear and love he propounds in the end the final truths, which must be finally observed but to which the world turns a deaf ear. These final rewards of iniquity and equity are the tortures of hell, which sprawls below and the delights of paradise, which soars above. From those tortures may he free us, his suppliants, and to these delights may he exalt us, his lovers, for he is the supreme good, the highest good, the heart of hearts, Jesus, who is God blessed for ever. Amen.

CISTERCIAN PUBLICATIONS INC.

Kalamazoo, Michigan

Texts and Studies
in the
Monastic Tradition

Temporarily out of print   † Forthcoming

THE CISTERCIAN STUDIES SERIES

Temporarily out of print   †*Forthcoming*

* *Temporarily out of print*　　　　　　† *Forthcoming*

Eight Chapters on Perfection and Angel's Song
(Walter Hilton)

Creative Suffering (Iulia de Beausobre)

Bringing Forth Christ. Five Feasts of the Child
Jesus (St Bonaventure)

Gentleness in St John of the Cross

Distributed in North America only for Fairacres Press.

DISTRIBUTED BOOKS

St Benedict: Man with An Idea (Melbourne Studies)

The Spirit of Simplicity

Benedict's Disciples (David Hugh Farmer)

The Emperor's Monk: A Contemporary Life of
Benedict of Aniane

A Guide to Cistercian Scholarship (2nd ed.)

*North American customers may order
through booksellers or directly
from the publisher:*

Cistercian Publications
WMU Station
Kalamazoo, Michigan 49008
(616) 383-4985

*Cistercian Publications are available in
Britain, Europe and the Common-
wealth through A. R. Mowbray &
Co Ltd   St Thomas House   Oxford
OX1 1SJ.
For a sterling price list, please consult
Mowbray's General Catalogue.*

*A complete catalogue of texts-in-
translation and studies on early,
medieval, and modern Christian
monasticism is available at no cost
from Cistercian Publications.*

*Cistercian monks and nuns have been
living lives of prayer & praise, meditation &
manual labor since the twelfth century.
They are part of an unbroken tradition
which extends back to the fourth century
and which continues today in the Catholic
church, the Orthodox churches, the
Anglican communion, and, most recently,
in the Protestant churches.*

*Share their way of life and their search for
God by reading Cistercian Publications.*